Sands to skylines

Rishi Mendez

Sands To Skylines

Rishi Mendez

Published by Rishi Mendez, 2024.

While every precaution has been taken in the preparation of this book, the publisher assumes no responsibility for errors or omissions, or for damages resulting from the use of the information contained herein.

SANDS TO SKYLINES

First edition. November 7, 2024.

Copyright © 2024 Rishi Mendez.

ISBN: 979-8230271277

Written by Rishi Mendez.

PROLOGUE

Sands to Skylines explores life as it will be experienced for an expat in the Gulf States , an orientation into the Gulf city life , highlighting the Persian Gulf's ancient beauty , transformation and modern Renaissance . While tracing the beautiful heritage of the desert life echoed in eternity , this book walks one through the path of the Gulf States desert roots and emerald oases to the global heights and success the region has achieved today . The Gulf's timeless journey continues as a story of beauty , legacy and change .

CHAPTERS

CHAPTER ONE

ORIENTATION

A First Glimpse of Life in the Gulf

Arriving in a Gulf country is like stepping into a world that balances between centuries-old traditions and cutting-edge modernity. For many, this region brings to mind images of vast deserts, towering skyscrapers, and flamboyant lifestyles. But beyond the shimmering city skylines and bustling traditional souks lies the real Gulf experience, which can only be understood by living and breathing the region's unique rhythms while you experience it firsthand.

For expatriates, the Gulf represents opportunities for for work, education, or business. It's a place where the dreams of millions converge, from the seasoned professional seeking a new challenge , medium skilled workers seeking an honest life to the unskilled worker pursuing a livelihood . While the dazzling growth and wealth are ever-present, the path to success in a Gulf country is neither instant nor simple. It requires resilience, hard work , cultural sensitivity, and most of all adaptability.

The six Gulf states, under the Gulf cooperation Council have transformed into a global magnet , from humble trading hubs to some of the world's most prosperous nations. Fueled by oil wealth and strategic investment, they've positioned themselves as global magnets for universal talent, attracting people from all corners of the world. In some Gulf states, expatriates make up a sizable percent of the population, creating a dynamic melting pot of nationalities, skills , languages, and cultures.

But for all the appeal , the Gulf remains a place of contrasts. While the cities boast incredible modern infrastructure, strict societal norms and deep-rooted cultural traditions still hold strong in the Gulf States . It is a region where innovation somehow coexists with conservatism, where the traditional Arab majlis (social gathering) can be found just a short distance from cutting-edge tech hubs or mega-malls.

One of the first things you'll notice about life in the Gulf is the climate. With its long, sweltering summers and mild winters, its unique climate is the heartbeat of the desert . The heat is a constant companion in summer . The thermometer often surpasses 40°C (104°F), and stepping outside feels like walking into an oven. But for Gulf locals and expatriates alike, the heat and sometimes humidity has become an integral part of life in the Gulf , something to endure and adapt to rather than avoid. Offices , public spaces and private residences are all kept cool by constant air conditioning and if one avoids going outdoors during the hottest hours of the day , it's manageable one can say . Nevertheless, it's recommended that your first trip to the Gulf , be scheduled to avoid the hottest three summer months , June , July and August , if possible . This may be advised to avoid the climate contrast shock and also , arriving in other months will give one an opportunity to seamlessly blend in with the climate in a gradual pace .

The desert, though seemingly barren, is not without its charm. Gulf citizens hold a deep respect for the land and its timeless silence. In fact, many Gulf nationals have a strong connection to their roots, which stretch back to the nomadic tribes that wandered these sands long before oil wealth transformed the whole region. This connection to the land can still be seen in the way people gather for weekend camping trips into the desert or take part in traditional falconry and camel racing.

A majority of expatriates come to the Gulf for work, looking for tax-free salaries and the promise of a higher standard of living. Yet, the working culture here can be different from what you might expect. Workweeks typically run from Sunday to Thursday, with Friday, the Islamic holy day, serving as the main day of rest. UAE follows a different weekend .

Gulf-based companies operate on Western models, but the pace of work and the value placed on relationships may require some adjustment. You will come to know that time moves differently in the Gulf, with meetings and negotiations often stretching beyond the scheduled office hours. Building personal connections and trust is very crucial to getting things done, whether you're working in a multinational corporation or managing a small business.

For professionals in the Gulf, understanding the importance of hierarchy and respecting local customs is essential. There is a strong emphasis on formality, and many decisions, particularly in larger companies or governmental bodies, must go through several layers of hierarchy for approval. Patience and persistence are key here for an ideal work life balance , so to speak .

Perhaps the most important aspect of life in the Gulf is understanding and respecting local culture. For that there should be a high degree of cultural awareness, whereby, one can integrate into the host country sooner .The region is deeply influenced by Islam religion which is adopted as the main religion in the Gulf countries , and the local way of life revolves around religious practices. Five times a day, the call to prayer echoes across all Gulf cities, reminding Muslims to stop what they're doing and focus on their faith. Non Muslim expatriates, are expected to respect this rhythm with courtesy.

Modesty in dress, especially for women, is an essential part of life in many Gulf states. While foreigners are not required to cover their heads or wear traditional dress, conservative attire is highly appreciated in public spaces. You'll quickly notice the unspoken rules about what is appropriate , as modesty and respect are emphasized widely in these states , in both appearance and behavior.

Additionally, relationships between men and women are viewed rather differently. Public displays of affection are frowned upon, and it is essential to be aware of how interactions may be interpreted by the others . In the Gulf, even small gestures can carry significant meaning.

It's to be commended that Gulf States also offer expatriates a supportive and diverse community of their own. Given the large number of foreign workers, most Gulf states are home to numerous expatriate social clubs, schools, and cultural organizations that cater to people from various backgrounds. From British, Indian, and Filipino communities to Americans, South Africans, and Australians, the region is a mosaic of people who are far from their native home but working to build a life here.

One of the greatest advantages for expatriates in the Gulf is the ability to maintain a lifestyle that might otherwise be out of reach in several other countries . Salaries are often competitive, and the absence of income tax means many workers can spend significantly while they live in these states The Gulf's penchant for luxury and convenience also means the more fortunate expatriates have access to high-end housing, international cuisine, and specialized healthcare. Shopping malls with designer brands, pricey international schools, and world-class entertainment have all become part of the fabric of daily life.

What you need to know about rules and regulations is that , it's essential to note that the Gulf States are all governed by a strict legal system, some if them based on a combination of Sharia (Islamic law) and civil law. Though the rules are clear, they can be significantly different from those in ones native country . Drinking alcohol, for example, is either restricted or totally banned in some Gulf states , and in some countries, obtaining a license is required to purchase or consume it. Drug offenses are treated with zero tolerance however , and punishments can be severe.

In addition, the Gulf operates on a system of sponsorship, meaning that expatriates require a local sponsor, either an individual or company, to live and work there. This sponsorship system ties workers to their employers, and leaving a job often requires permission from the sponsor to transfer to another company or leave the country. It's crucial to understand the legalities of contracts, sponsorship, and residency visas before arriving to work in the Gulf.

Despite the challenges, the Gulf remains a land of opportunity and beauty with the charm of its new Metropolitan cities and timeless deserts . It's a place where careers can flourish, where cultural exchanges happen daily, and where innovation is shaping the future of the region. Whether you're drawn by the economic potential, the rich cultural tapestry, or the chance to experience a different way of life, if the rules are abided by , the Gulf offers a unique experience.

Life here requires balance . By understanding and embracing local customs while carving out your own space in a diverse and fast evolving landscape. Those who succeed in the Gulf States are the ones who approach it with respect, hard work , an open mind, and the willingness to adapt to its unique blend of tradition and progress.

Preparing for life in the Gulf requires both practical and cultural readiness. One of the first steps is to familiarize yourself with the specific country's visa and residency policies, as each Gulf nation has its own requirements and processes. Ensure that your work visa is sponsored by a reputable employer, and clarify the terms of your employment contract, especially regarding benefits like housing, healthcare if any , and annual leave. It's also advisable to set up your finances before moving by opening an international bank account if necessary and research the cost of living, including accommodation, transportation, food and utilities, which can vary significantly depending on the city. Having some savings set aside for emergencies, especially when first settling in, can provide extra security and peace of mind .

Understanding the cultural dress codes, behaviors, and religious practices such as prayer times or fasting during Ramadan is essential. While many expatriate communities thrive in some Gulf cities cities like Dubai and Abu Dhabi, that allow for a more liberal lifestyle, it is important to respect the rules governing public conduct, particularly around gender interaction and alcohol consumption. Additionally, one should be ready for climate-related challenges, as the extreme heat in summer can affect daily life, especially for those coming from other cooler climates. Engaging with other expatriates, joining social groups, and learning basic Arabic phrases can also help ease the transition and assist to blend in quickly and enrich your experience in the Gulf.

As you embark on your journey, remember that the Gulf is not just about what it offers financially or professionally. It's also about what it can teach you. Life here teaches one about patience, tolerance, and the beauty of living in a place like no other , where history and the future intertwine in every moment

CHAPTER 2

JOB SCENE , THE REALITY

Focusing on the job scenes in Gulf countries for skilled, medium-skilled, and unskilled workers , this could be divided into the following sections. A detailed breakdown is below which will give a clear idea of the current jobs in demand and what's required of candidates who chose to live in the gulf .

Navigating the Job Market in Gulf Countries and has multiple opportunities and equally if not more challenges . The Gulf Cooperation Council (GCC) countries—comprising are renowned for their lucrative job markets. The region attracts millions of expatriates from across the globe seeking better career prospects, tax-free income, and high living standards. However, the truth is that the opportunities and challenges differ greatly depending on one's skill level and it hinges greatly on one's skill level , skilled, medium-skilled, or unskilled. This chapter attempts to delve into the distinct experiences faced by workers across these categories.

You could say that skilled labor pays the highest . But the job openings for this high income category is several times lower in volume than the semi skilled or unskilled . One could say that they are the professions in high demand . Skilled labor refers to jobs requiring specialized knowledge, more advanced and longer education, or technical training. Positions in healthcare, IT, engineering, finance, aviation and education fall under this category. These roles are often filled by majority of expatriates from Western countries, India, the Philippines, and other parts of Asia. Industries employing them are Oil & Gas , Construction & Infrastructure , Healthcare , Education , Information Technology and Aviation . Their roles fill the market need for engineering , geology , civil engineering, architecture, projects refinery , software development, data science, IT , marketing , transport and logistics, medicine. , pharmaceuticals , professors and teachers .

The Gulf states offer high-paying positions for all above professionals, particularly in industries like energy, health , finance, aviation and IT. Government initiatives such as the UAE's push for a knowledge-based economy and future cities planned by the Gulf states are driving demand for talent in emerging fields like AI, renewable energy, and cybersecurity.

The challenges faced by professionals are mainly seen in the Work - Life Balance . The expectations are very high resulting in long working hours until the desired result is obtained . This fast paced competitive environment in fast developing Gulf cities can lead to burnout. Contract rigidity is seen widely . Contracts may include clauses that restrict movement between employers and countries, limiting flexibility.

This current demand for skilled , and semi skilled personnel will see a decline in coming years as localization policies are already coming into effect . Increasing number of skilled and semi skilled jobs are being reserved for the local citizens. Some Gulf countries are pushing for this very strongly to encourage the local population to take over jobs , to ultimately stop the need to depend on outside labor by requiring a certain percentage of jobs to go to locals, which could reduce expatriate opportunities to a very large extent . Gulf countries are rapidly enforcing this in the government sectors first , where lately a large volume of expatriate labor have been replaced by local graduates .

Medium skilled Labour , however has been bridging the gap . Medium-skilled workers include technicians, mechanics, sales staff, mid-level administrators , and Human Resources experts in fields of marketing , construction and maintenance . The hospitality and retail industry employs a huge number of sales associates , chefs and hotel managers . In addition to this are the manufacturing sector , employing machine operators and production and quality controllers . The transport and logistics sector has seen a huge demand for drivers , warehouse managers and supply chain coordinators

These roles require vocational training or a diploma but don't necessarily need a university degree. If they know their job , with varied language skills including English , then their roles are made somewhat bearable .This group forms a large part of the expatriate workforce, with many workers coming from countries like India, Pakistan, Nepal, other Arab countries and the Philippines.

The most opportunities seen in the Gulf states lately , are in real estate, retail, aviation and hospitality sectors , which are expanding, driven by mega-projects such as hosting international sporting events , building future visionary cities , construction of newer better airports , efficient projects and to top it all the constant demand of travel related products for the local population as well as the expatriates who have to shuttle back and forth between their countries . Workers in these sectors can find steady employment with decent wages for a long time to come

There are challenges faced , that include work permits and visa renewals Renewals can be a complex and bureaucratic process. Many workers rely on company sponsorships, and changing employers may result in losing their visa status.Medium-skilled workers often face significant wage disparities compared to their skilled counterparts, despite working the same or more long hours.Housing Conditions are challenging in some areas . While some companies offer decent accommodation, many workers who are not in self obtained rentals endure crowded and uncomfortable living arrangements.

Unskilled Labor the next category can be rightly called the backbone of Gulf Economies . Unskilled labor refers to jobs that don't require formal education or specialized training. Most of these workers are employed in construction, laborers , cleaners , helpers ,domestic work, nannies , housemaids , gardeners , farmers , shepherds or other physically demanding fields. The municipalities of these countries also employ street cleaners , porters , and janitors in government and private institutions . tea huge demand is seen in the restaurant and fast food industry where thousands are employed as baristas , waiters , in specialized food , regular food as well as fast food preparation The majority come from South Asia and Southeast Asia, with India, few Arab countries , Bangladesh, Sri Lanka , Pakistan, and Nepal being the top suppliers of labor to the Gulf.

Despite the physically demanding nature of the jobs, unskilled workers can earn considerably more in the Gulf than they could in their home countries. Many come to the region on fixed contracts ranging from two to five years, sending remittances back home to support their families.

Challenges faced by all workers , skilled semi skilled or unskilled is the Kamala System , which means sponsorship . Workers are employed under the Kafala system, which ties their legal and employment status to their employers. This system has been criticized for giving employers excessive control over workers, leading to exploitation in some cases.

Working Conditions especially in summer are tough . Construction and domestic workers often face harsh working conditions. Laborers endure extreme heat and long hours, while domestic workers may experience isolation, verbal, or physical abuse. Lately some countries have imposed laws to protect workers during the scorching heat of the summer . That was welcomed all over the region.

While some countries have made reforms to improve labor laws, there remains a lack of robust legal protections for unskilled workers, especially for domestic help.Legal Frameworks and Labor Rights and reforms were made in recent years which have made some progress . So there have been significant reforms aimed at improving labor conditions, particularly in Qatar and the UAE. Qatar abolished the exit permit requirement and introduced a minimum wage law, while the UAE has focused on worker housing standards and improved wage protection systems.

Still a long way to go , it may be noted . Despite these efforts, challenges remain, especially in terms of implementation and enforcement. Human rights organizations continue to report cases of wage theft, passport confiscation, and forced labor across the Gulf , which are still very much rampant .

Living Conditions for all categories of workers are actually a spectrum of Experiences . Top skilled workers , most receive housing allowances or company-provided accommodations in high-end gated communities or urban apartments. Skilled professionals often enjoy a cosmopolitan lifestyle in cities like Dubai, Abu Dhabi, and Doha with ample amenities for an active social life . But that's not the case for all skilled workers in the Gulf .

Regarding semi skilled workers across the Gulf Many live in rented or shared apartments, often located in mid-range urban districts. While they have access to better amenities than unskilled workers, they may still face issues like overcrowding and high rents .

Unskilled workers typically live in labor camps owned by the respective company that recruited them , sometimes in harsh conditions. Some companies do provide apartments with are ample space and with enough living space . Whereas others who bring workers to work on huge projects typically have overcrowded living spaces . Access to recreational activities and social interaction is often very limited, contributing to a sense of isolation , depression and loneliness . Social media however , provides some relief for the workers as they can connect to home daily, provided they are provided with an internet connection .

Cultural Adjustments are very much needed for an expatriate workforce to survive in the Gulf . All workers, regardless of skill level, must navigate cultural differences, whether it's adapting to conservative social norms in one state or balancing the multicultural but fast-paced environment in other states .

So what's the future outlook . What lies ahead regarding expatriate jobs . As the Gulf economies diversify away from oil, the demand for skilled labor in technology, healthcare, aviation , logistics and education is expected to grow. At the same time, with automation threatening low-skilled jobs, the future of unskilled and even medium-skilled workers could become more precarious. However, major projects like Neom in Saudi Arabia and continued growth in tourism, retail, and real estate will still require a significant expatriate workforce for years to come.

The Gulf job market presents unique opportunities for workers across all skill levels. However, the benefits come with challenges, particularly for unskilled and medium-skilled laborers. While progress is being made in labor reforms, understanding the legal frameworks, navigating cultural differences, and preparing for the rigors of life in the Gulf are key to making the most of one's time working in the region.

When seeking employment in the Gulf countries, thorough preparation is key. Start by researching the specific industry you aim to enter and understanding the demand for your skill level, whether skilled, medium-skilled, or unskilled. It's important to tailor your resume and highlight relevant experience and qualifications that match the job market in the Gulf. Networking through online professional platforms like LinkedIn, industry-specific forums, company websites , employee reviews or expat groups can also help in gaining valuable insights or even potential job leads. Additionally, be mindful of local labor laws, visa requirements, and the terms of your employment contract before committing to a job offer. Understanding these can prevent future legal or financial challenges, such as issues with visa renewals or restrictions on changing employers.

Once you've secured a job, prepare for the cultural and social differences you may encounter in Gulf countries. While major cities like Dubai and Doha are cosmopolitan, the Gulf as a whole tends to be more conservative, Respect for local customs and laws is crucial, both in professional and personal settings. It's also beneficial to plan your living arrangements, taking into consideration the cost of living, housing provided by your employer, and the quality of healthcare and education if you are relocating with family. Job seekers should also have a clear financial plan, factoring in possible expenses for renewing visas, medical insurance, education bills or emergency travel back home.

CHAPTER 3

EDUCATION OPTIONS IN THE GULF CITIES

Understanding the school education system's in Gulf Countries is very important if one is planning to work there while relocating with family . As in most countries , there are Public schools run by the government , and private schools which are mostly owned by individuals or as a corporate , family run institution

Education in the Gulf Cooperation Council (GCC) countries has undergone significant transformation over the past few decades. With rising populations and a growing expatriate workforce, the demand for quality education has increased in both public and private sectors. However, the experiences and educational systems can vary widely between local citizens and expatriates. This chapter explores the structure, curriculum, and challenges of both government-run and privately owned schools in the Gulf countries, giving parents and educators a clearer understanding of the opportunities and limitations before setting up a life there .

The Government School Systems offer mostly education for Local Citizens . Public schools in the Gulf are primarily intended for local citizens and, in some cases, children of Gulf nationals or government employees. These schools are fully funded by the respective state and are often free of charge for nationals. The medium of instruction is predominantly Arabic, with a heavy focus on Islamic studies, Arab history, and local culture, together with languages , science and mathematics .

Public schools follow national curricula, which vary slightly between the Gulf countries but share mostly common themes of Arab culture, Islamic studies, and national identity. Key subjects include Arabic, mathematics, science, and social studies, along with a strong emphasis on religious education. English is taught as a second language, but proficiency levels can vary between country to country .

Education is mostly compulsory for children between the ages of 6 and 15. The curriculum is strictly regulated by the Ministry of Education, focusing on Islamic principles alongside secular subjects. In the UAE , Public schools are increasingly adopting modern teaching methods and digital learning. However Arabic remains the main medium of instruction, with English introduced gradually.

In Qatar , and Bahrain , Public schools emphasize Arabic, Islamic studies, and patriotism, with Qatar introducing reforms in recent years to improve science and technology education.

While government schools are well-funded, they have faced challenges related to teacher quality, particularly in subjects like English and science. The curriculum is also seen as heavily traditional, with some criticism that it does not fully prepare students for global competitiveness or modern employment markets. Another major challenge is the language barrier for expatriate children, as public schools teach in Arabic, making them less attractive or just inaccessible to non-Arabic-speaking families.

Private School Systems , the majority of them are Catering to Expatriates and also the wealthier elites , with costs varying from school to school . They are also patronized by the local wealthy families in the gulf who seek a different education model .

These schools are diverse, offering a range of curricula, including British, American, International Baccalaureate (IB), Indian, and French systems. The medium of instruction in private schools is typically English and sometimes another foreign language, depending on the curriculum followed.

Private schools vary widely , in that they provide families with options that align with their home country's education system or international standards. Some of the most popular curricula include , British Curriculum (IGCSE and A-Levels) . They are Widely followed and is a preferred choice for local citizens in all the Gulf countries . British schools offer a structured path with standardized exams that are internationally recognized , with the fees being on a higher scale .

American Curriculum . This curriculum is known for its flexibility, American international schools emphasize continuous assessment, with students following a broad curriculum before taking SAT or ACT exams. They are also widely popular in the Gulf . They cost on a higher scale too.

International Baccalaureate (IB) . Offering a globally recognized program, IB schools focus on critical thinking, creativity, and a well-rounded education. They are popular among expatriates seeking international qualifications for their children.

Indian Curriculum (CBSE and ICSE) . Highly popular among the large Indian expatriate community in all Gulf states , where they are present since a long time , Indian schools follow a rigorous academic program focusing on English , science, mathematics, and other languages.

Private schools offer a globalized education that often provides opportunities for extracurricular activities, state-of-the-art facilities, and better teacher-student ratios. The international nature of these schools allows expatriate children to continue their education seamlessly when moving between countries. Additionally, private schools are more likely to offer bilingual or English-medium education, making them an appealing choice for expatriate families.

One of the biggest challenges in all the private school sectors is cost. Fees can be prohibitively high, particularly in premium schools that offer international curricula or elite-level education. Parents must also consider additional expenses, such as school uniforms, textbooks, and extracurricular activities. Another concern is the wide variation in the quality of education, with some private schools reportedly offering substandard facilities and unqualified teachers, particularly in lower-tier schools. Regulation and oversight can be inconsistent, and parents are encouraged to do thorough research before enrolling their children , once you are relocated .

The Role of Government Reforms in Education and modern visions are changing . Several Gulf countries are making significant reforms to enhance both public and private education systems. Governments are investing in new technologies, teacher training, and modern curricula to meet global standards and prepare students for the future workforce.

The UAE for example has prioritized innovation in education, promoting STEM (science, technology, engineering, and mathematics) subjects and adopting smart learning initiatives. In recent years, the government has launched initiatives to encourage bilingualism, improving Arabic proficiency alongside English.

Other Gulf countries also have undertaken sweeping reforms, focusing on reducing reliance on oil and building a knowledge-based economy. Education is a key component of these efforts, with a renewed emphasis on English proficiency, technical skills, and entrepreneurship in schools.

The aim is to develop a world-class education system by enhancing its public schools and attracting prestigious international institutions. The Gulf countries have also focused on integrating digital learning and promoting research-based education , especially in Qatar .

Despite the enthusiasm for reform, there are significant challenges in implementing changes across vast and diverse school systems . Teacher quality, outdated infrastructure, and bureaucratic hurdles often slow the pace of progress. In public schools, the focus remains on preserving local traditions and culture, which can sometimes conflict with the push for modernization. Furthermore, for private schools, maintaining affordable tuition fees while implementing international standards remains a difficult balance even today .

The Expatriate education experience however starts with the attempt to access to schools for their children . For expatriate families, one of the major considerations when relocating to the Gulf is finding suitable schools for their children. Private international schools are the primary option for most expats since public schools are geared toward local citizens and teach in Arabic. As a result, the demand for private school places is high, particularly in major cities like Dubai, Abu Dhabi, Doha, and Riyadh.

Taking into consideration all the above , one of the advantages of living in the Gulf is the diversity of educational options available to expatriate families. Whether parents prefer the British, American, or IB system, or want their children to follow a curriculum from their home country, they are likely to find a school that meets their needs. Many schools also offer robust after-school programs and facilities, such as sports, arts, and language clubs, which enrich the overall learning experience.

Challenges for expat parents are high tuition fees and long waiting lists for popular schools . Some employers offer education allowances as part of relocation packages, but these may not cover the full cost of tuition, especially at prestigious international schools. Additionally, some expatriates may struggle with cultural differences in the education system, particularly in countries with more conservative social norms, where gender segregation or limitations on extracurricular activities may apply.

Future outlook for education in the Gulf, seems to be to shift towards a Knowledge-Based Economy . The Gulf region's focus on diversifying its economy away from oil is driving a renewed commitment to education, particularly in STEM fields. There is an increasing emphasis on preparing students for the global workforce, promoting critical thinking, and nurturing entrepreneurship from a young age. As governments continue to invest in education, more international schools are expected to open, especially in countries like UAE , Saudi Arabia and Qatar, where foreign investment and development projects are driving population growth.

Impact of Technology on Learning can be seen after the COVID-19 pandemic , which accelerated the adoption of digital learning tools, and many schools have continued to integrate online platforms and smart learning technologies into their curriculums. This shift towards blended learning , combining in-person and virtual education , may shape the future of education in the Gulf, particularly in urban areas where access to technology is widespread.

Education in the Gulf is a complex and evolving landscape, offering both opportunities and challenges for local citizens and expatriates alike. While public schools focus on preserving cultural values and Islamic teachings, private schools provide a diverse range of international curricula catering to the global expat population. With ongoing government reforms and investments in the education sector, the Gulf is positioning itself to build a well-educated, globally competitive workforce for the future. Understanding the differences between public and private schools, as well as the educational reforms in place, is essential for parents, educators, and policymakers shaping the future of learning in the region.

This chapter outlined the current educational landscape in the Gulf, offering a comprehensive look at both government and private school systems, the challenges they face, and the ongoing efforts to improve education across the region.

CHAPTER 4

HOUSING SYSTEMS , WHAT TO EXPECT

This chapter details the housing systems prevalent in the Gulf states for an expatriate and those followed by the locals , for a contrast . The housing landscape in the Gulf countries is a unique mix of traditional and government-subsidized accommodations for locals and a diverse range of rental properties catering to expatriates. Each Gulf nation offers different housing models, with some countries, like the United Arab Emirates and Qatar, recently focusing heavily on luxury and high-end properties with the aim of attracting investors , while all the other Gulf states offer more varied rental only options.

This chapter also explores the key types of accommodations, government housing policies, and the challenges faced by residents. For a contrast we will mention here that housing for all Gulf citizens are supported by the respective government and are for mostly sprawling traditional homes owned individually . In most Gulf countries they benefit from programs designed to provide affordable and comfortable living spaces. These schemes are part of larger social welfare systems aimed at ensuring that the local population, particularly those from mid income groups, have access to quality housing.

Additionally, many locals prefer to live in traditional family homes, often located in suburban or semi-urban areas, which reflect their cultural values and familial ties. Gulf governments have implemented various subsidized housing programs to assist their citizens. These include interest-free loans, subsidies for home purchases, and in some cases, free plots of land for building homes.

The goal is to help locals, especially young families, to own property and promote long-term residency in their home country.

In UAE for example , The government offers housing loans, grants, and free land to Emirati citizens through the Sheikh Zayed Housing Program. Many citizens take advantage of these schemes to build spacious villas in residential suburbs, often in close proximity to their extended family members.

In Saudi Arabia , it's noted that Ministry of Housing provides various support options to Saudi citizens, including low-cost housing units and home ownership programs under the Sakani initiative, which offers financial assistance, housing loans, and the allocation of land for residential use.

In Qatar , The Qatar Development Bank provides citizens with affordable loans for home construction, while the government allocates plots of land in designated areas for Qatari families. The other Gulf States too , follow similar patterns .

In addition to owning modern housing developments, many locals continue to live in large traditional family homes, which are often multi-generational and spacious. These homes reflect the Gulf's cultural emphasis on family ties and privacy. Most are standalone villas with multiple bedrooms, separate living spaces for men and women, and large outdoor areas. In more rural areas, traditional homes may still follow the architectural styles of the past, such as the use of courtyards, high walls, and wind towers designed to provide natural ventilation in the hot climate.

Although government-supported housing is widespread, challenges exist like long waiting lists for certain programs, which can delay access to housing for young families. Furthermore, as populations grow, there is increasing pressure on urban infrastructure, pushing some locals to seek homes further away from city centers, leading to longer commutes and challenges related to urban sprawl in Gulf countries .

Housing for Expatriates are closely tied to the rental market and shared living arrangements . Expatriates, who make up a significant portion of the population in many Gulf countries, have a wide range of rental only housing options, from luxury apartments in city centers to more affordable accommodation in the outskirts and suburbs . Unlike locals, expatriates do not have access to government-subsidized housing and rely primarily on the private rental market. Housing prices can vary significantly based on location, amenities, and proximity to work hubs, with expatriates generally renting homes for the duration of their stay only .

Types of Expat Housing used Luxury Apartments and High-Rises: In cities like Dubai, Abu Dhabi, Doha, and Manama, wealthy expatriates often choose to live in high-rise apartment buildings equipped with modern amenities such as gyms, swimming pools, and 24/7 security. These properties are typically located in upscale neighborhoods or near business districts, offering convenience but at a rather high premium price. For example, areas like Dubai Marina and The Pearl-Qatar cater to wealthy expatriates and offer a very luxurious lifestyle.

In contrast , Many skilled and medium skilled expatriates, especially those with families, prefer renting medium villas in gated communities. These villas offer more space, privacy, and are often located in suburban areas. In countries like the UAE and Qatar, these communities may also include parks, schools, health centers and retail centers, making them ideal for family living. Examples of popular villa communities include Arabian Ranches in Dubai and Al Waab in Doha

For expatriates seeking more affordable options, mid-range apartments and townhouses are available in suburban areas or less central locations. These properties are typically smaller and may offer fewer amenities but remain comfortable and well-maintained. Examples are areas such as Al Barsha in Dubai or Al Sadd in Doha provide a balance between affordability and the same time easy proximity to city centers.

Regarding housing costs and leasing terms , you may note that renting a property as an expatriate in the Gulf generally involves signing a lease for one year, with rent often paid upfront in one or sometimes two installments, although some landlords accept monthly or quarterly payments. Rent prices vary considerably depending on the country and city. For instance, rent in Dubai and Doha tends to be more expensive than in Muscat or Manama. While expatriates with higher incomes can afford luxury apartments and villas, those with lower incomes often settle in mid-range or budget accommodations , which still offer clean maintained living spaces .Each of these apartment buildings typically have a care taker to maintain and generally see to the upkeep of the building .

Additionally, many employers but not all , in the Gulf offer housing allowances as part of their employment packages, particularly for mid-level and senior expatriates. This is a common benefit, especially in industries like oil and gas, construction, and finance. Some companies even provide fully furnished accommodation, either in company-owned housing or rented apartments, reducing the burden on expatriates to find housing independently.

One of the primary challenges for expatriates in the Gulf is the cost of housing, which can be disproportionately high compared to income, particularly in premium locations. In some cities, high demand for certain types of housing has led to price inflation, making it difficult for middle-income expatriates to afford central accommodations. Additionally, expatriates must be mindful of the terms of their lease, including maintenance responsibilities, utility payments, and penalties for early termination, as these vary widely between landlords and can lead to disputes. It can be said that rental and utility costs swallow up a lion share of expatriate incomes.

Key Considerations for Expats while renting homes in the Gulf, is the need to be aware of the legal frameworks governing housing. In most Gulf countries, strict regulations govern property leases, ownership, and disputes. Expatriates, in particular, need to understand what is their clear rights as tenants, as rental agreements can be complex. For example, Dubai has introduced the Rental Dispute Settlement Centre to address disputes between landlords and tenants.

In certain areas of the Gulf, expatriates are now allowed to purchase property, though this is usually restricted to designated freehold areas. In Dubai, for instance, expatriates can buy property in freehold zones like Downtown Dubai, while in Bahrain, expats can own property in areas like Amwaj Islands. However, purchasing property comes with its own set of legal and financial challenges, and expats are advised to carefully review the rules and regulations before investing their money in a foreign land.

Housing in the Gulf is shaped by local customs and cultural expectations. For locals, family life and privacy are paramount, influencing the design and layout of homes. Expats living in villa communities or suburban areas may also experience cultural practices such as gender segregation in some neighborhoods or expectations around modest dress and behavior. Understanding and respecting these cultural norms is key to a harmonious living experience in the Gulf States.

Coming to the future trends in Gulf Housing, Governments are taking Initiatives for large scale Urban Development. . With growing populations and expanding urban areas, Gulf countries are investing in large-scale housing and infrastructure projects. Governments are increasingly focused on sustainable urban development, integrating smart technologies, and expanding affordable housing options for both locals and expatriates.

In cities like Dubai and Doha, new residential areas are being developed with a focus on eco-friendly practices, including energy-efficient buildings and public transportation networks incorporating Sustainability and Green Living . Sustainability is in fact becoming a critical factor in the future of housing in the Gulf. With high energy consumption due to the region's extreme climate conditions in summer , governments and developers are working to incorporate green technologies such as solar panels, energy-efficient cooling systems, and water recycling in new residential developments. Initiatives like Abu Dhabi's Masdar City, is a city planned and designed to be carbon-neutral, are examples of how the region is moving toward sustainable living solutions.

The emerging trend of minimalistic modular homes in the Gulf region represents a significant shift in housing design and construction, prioritizing efficiency, sustainability, and affordability. These homes are typically prefabricated and constructed off-site, allowing for faster assembly and reduced waste compared to traditional building methods. The minimalist aesthetic not only emphasizes clean lines and open spaces but also focuses on maximizing functionality in smaller living areas. This approach is particularly appealing in urban settings where land is scarce and expensive, making modular homes an attractive option for both expatriates and locals seeking modern, efficient living solutions.

Governments and developers in the Gulf are increasingly recognizing the benefits of modular construction as a way to address housing shortages and promote sustainable living. Initiatives to encourage the adoption of modular homes include partnerships with innovative design firms and investments in smart home technologies that enhance energy efficiency.

For example, in the UAE, projects like The Sustainable City have showcased how modular homes can integrate renewable energy sources, such as solar panels, and utilize water-saving technologies. As urban populations continue to grow, the minimalistic modular home trend not only provides a viable solution for affordable housing but also aligns with the Gulf's broader goals of sustainability and environmental stewardship.

The Sustainable City in the UAE, located in Dubai, thus is undoubtedly a pioneering development designed to showcase sustainable living and environmental responsibility. Launched by Diamond Developers, this community aims to integrate sustainability into everyday life through innovative design, energy-efficient technologies, and affordable eco-friendly practices.

These types of community constructions consists of average around 500 villas and apartments built using sustainable materials and techniques. The design emphasizes natural ventilation and features abundant green spaces, incorporating features like shaded walkways, gardens, and open-air spaces to promote outdoor living.

Sustainable cities are powered by renewable energy sources, primarily solar power. Each home is equipped with solar panels, enabling residents to generate their own electricity and reduce reliance on the grid. The development aims for net-zero energy consumption, with excess energy fed back into the community grid.

A key aspect of sustainability is efficient water management. The community employs advanced irrigation systems that utilize recycled wastewater for landscaping. This not only conserves water but also supports the lush greenery throughout the development.

Sustainable Cities promotes eco-friendly green mobility transportation options. Electric vehicle charging stations are available, and the community is designed for walkability, encouraging residents to use bicycles or walk instead of relying on cars. The use of autonomous electric shuttles is also being explored to enhance mobility within the community.

The development fosters a strong sense of community life style like exists in their home countries , through shared spaces, including parks, playgrounds, and communal gardens. It also features amenities like a schools , and shopping areas , providing residents with essential services and promoting a healthy lifestyle.

Some communities even offer education on sustainability, offering workshops and programs for residents to learn about environmentally friendly practices. Schools within the community incorporate sustainability into their curricula, teaching children the importance of environmental stewardship.

The Sustainable Cities planned and some implemented by the Gulf States has gaineed recognition as a model for sustainable urban development in the Middle East, attracting attention from international organizations and governments. It serves as an inspiration for future developments in the region and showcases the potential for integrating sustainability into urban planning. By balancing modern living with environmental responsibility, The Sustainable Cities idea represents a forward-thinking approach to addressing the challenges of urbanization and climate change in the Gulf.

Doha has notably completed several modular home projects, particularly focused on workers' accommodations. One significant project is the Mesaieed Industrial City Workers Accommodation , which was built to support 10,000 workers involved in the petrochemical and refinery sectors. This project utilized prefabricated modular structures and was completed as a turnkey solution by Dorce, a company experienced in modular construction in the region.

Additionally, modular housing has become a preferred choice for providing efficient and quick housing solutions in Qatar, aligning with the country's rapid development goals . Other Gulf states are catching up on the ideas of sustainable housing and we will see projects implemented in more Gulf States imminently

In conclusion , the housing systems in the Gulf reflect the region's diverse population and rapid economic development. For locals, government-supported housing provides a secure foundation for families, while expatriates navigate a competitive rental market with options ranging from luxurious villas to affordable apartments. Understanding the housing landscape , whether through government programs, private rentals, or expatriate communities , is essential for anyone considering relocating to or within the Gulf. As governments continue to modernize and expand their housing infrastructure, both locals and expatriates will benefit from more diverse and sustainable housing options in the years to come.

CHAPTER 5

HEALTHCARE FACILITIES

The healthcare infrastructure in the Gulf Cooperation Council (GCC) countries varies significantly between expatriates and citizens, shaped by factors like funding, availability of services, and regulatory frameworks.

Expatriates in the Gulf, particularly in countries like the UAE and Qatar, often rely on private healthcare providers due to the limited coverage of public healthcare for all services. Expatriates in all Gulf countries typically must secure annual health insurance too , which is often mandated by employers. The healthcare system in these countries is characterized by high-quality medical facilities and advanced technologies, making it appealing for expats. However, they can face challenges such as higher out-of-pocket expenses and limited access to public services, which are primarily designed for citizens.

In many GCC states, the healthcare sector heavily relies on expatriate skilled and medium skilled medical professionals. For instance, approximately 85% of the nursing workforce in the UAE is expatriate, leading to some challenges in continuity of care and healthcare delivery. Expatriates may also experience variations in the quality of care due to the diverse cultural backgrounds of healthcare providers, which can affect the consistency of services.

In contrast, GCC citizens generally have greater access to public healthcare services, which are wholly funded by the government. Citizens often receive free or subsidized healthcare, contributing to a healthcare system designed to serve national populations effectively. Governments invest heavily in building and maintaining hospitals, clinics, and specialized medical facilities.

Despite these advantages, many citizens in Gulf countries still opt for private healthcare services due to shorter wait times and perceived higher quality. The public sector is under strain from the increasing prevalence of non-communicable diseases (NCDs) and an aging local population, prompting reforms to improve service delivery and preventive care, especially geriatric and pediatric care .

Both expatriates and citizens face challenges within the GCC healthcare system, including high rates of NCDs, a shortage of local healthcare professionals, and rising healthcare and medication costs. Many Gulf states are now charging the expatriate population for clinic and hospital visits , diagnostic tests and all medications . This brings in a considerable amount of funds for these states . This being the case , many medium income expatriates who cannot afford medical consultation fees , rely on reputable pharmacies to obtain non prescription , over the counter medications . The region is actively pursuing reforms to transition from a reactive "find it and fix it" model to a more proactive system that focuses on preventive care. Investments in technology, such as e-health initiatives and electronic medical records, are also being made to enhance service efficiency and patient outcomes.

In summary, while expatriates in the Gulf benefit from advanced healthcare facilities and technologies, they often face barriers related to insurance and access. Citizens enjoy more comprehensive public healthcare services but are also impacted by systemic challenges. Both groups are at the forefront of ongoing reforms aimed at enhancing the overall healthcare landscape in the region.

Surgical care in the Gulf region has advanced significantly, particularly in the realm of robotic surgery. Countries like the UAE are becoming key players in this field, hosting major events like the Global Robotic MedTech Forum, which showcased cutting-edge technologies in minimally invasive surgery. This forum brought together leading experts and companies to discuss innovations like the XCath endovascular robot, designed to improve surgical outcomes and patient care.

The Gulf countries are investing heavily in healthcare infrastructure, with a focus on integrating advanced medical technologies. This is reflected in the increasing number of specialized clinics and hospitals offering robotic surgeries in certain Gulf countries . These surgeries guided by a surgeon , are noted for their precision and have reduced recovery times .

Furthermore, the interest in robotic surgery is supported by a robust healthcare system, government backing, and a desire to become a leader in medical technology innovation. As these advancements continue, patients in the Gulf region can expect improved access to state-of-the-art surgical care.

Family health clinics in the Gulf region play a crucial role in providing basic healthcare services, especially for seasonal ailments. These clinics, often part of national healthcare systems, offer a variety of services aimed at managing common health issues, including preventive care and vaccinations.

In Qatar, for instance, the Ministry of Public Health collaborates with the Primary Health Care Corporation and Hamad Medical Corporation to provide free seasonal flu vaccines at all primary health centers and selected private clinics. This initiative is particularly important given the overlapping symptoms of seasonal flu and COVID-19, emphasizing the need for vaccination to protect vulnerable populations, including children and the elderly.

Similarly, in the UAE, clinics often offer comprehensive services for common ailments, such as respiratory infections and gastrointestinal issues, which are prevalent during seasonal changes. Many of these clinics are well-equipped to provide preventive care, including vaccinations, health screenings, and educational resources on managing seasonal health issues.

Overall, family health clinics in the Gulf are vital for expats and citizens alike, providing accessible care for everyday health needs while promoting public health initiatives to tackle seasonal illnesses. For more detailed information on specific programs and services, checking with local health authorities or clinic and hospital websites is recommended.

CHAPTER 6

RELIGION

The Gulf region, which consists primarily of the six nations of the Gulf Cooperation Council (GCC) , represents one of the most important areas in the Islamic world. It is home to some of the most significant Islamic sites, including Mecca and Medina, and is a region where religion plays a central role in shaping social, political, and cultural life.

Islam has been the dominant faith in the Arabian Peninsula since the 7th century starting from Mecca. The religion quickly spread throughout the region, replacing polytheistic and animistic religions that had previously been practiced. The Gulf became a core part of the Muslim world, and over time, the influence of Islam in the region grew stronger and more complex, with various sects and schools of thought emerging.

Throughout its history, the Gulf has been shaped by the dynamics between the two main branches of Islam . Sunni and Shia. The majority of the Gulf population follows Sunni Islam, but significant Shia populations exist, particularly in Bahrain, eastern Saudi Arabia, and parts of Kuwait. This sectarian divide has often influenced political and social developments in the region.

The majority of the Gulf's population adheres to Sunni Islam. Within Sunni Islam, the predominant school of thought is the Hanbali school, which is known for its strict adherence to the teachings of the Quran and Hadith . The Hanbali school forms the foundation for the ultra-conservative puritanical movement that emerged in the 18 Th century known as Wahhabism, which has played a major role in shaping religious life in Saudi Arabia , becoming closely intertwined with the Saudi ruling family and, as a result, has heavily influenced Saudi governance, legal systems, and educational policies.

In other Gulf countries, while Wahhabism is less dominant, Islam still plays a crucial role in public life. In countries like the UAE , the Maliki and Shafi'i schools of Sunni thought have more influence. These schools are generally more flexible in their interpretations of Islamic law , particularly in areas related to trade and modern life.

While Sunni Islam dominates the Gulf, Shia Muslims form significant minorities, especially in Bahrain . Shia Muslims in the Gulf generally follow the Twelver Shia school . Although Shia communities in the Gulf have long faced social marginalization, currently they are all existing peacefully alongside the others .

In Oman, a distinctive form of Islam known as Ibadi Islam is the dominant sect. Ibadism, one of the oldest Islamic sects . It shares some similarities with Sunni Islam but differs in its approach to governance and community organization. The Ibadis are known for their tolerance of other religious sects and for their moderate views , which has shaped Oman's policies of neutrality and diplomacy in the region. Oman has maintained a policy of religious tolerance and moderation, allowing different Islamic sects and other religious communities to coexist peacefully. Religion plays a central role in Omani identity, but the state has largely avoided any sectarian tensions .

In the Gulf, the boundaries between religion and politics are often blurred, with religion serving as a key pillar of state legitimacy. The Saudi monarchy is the guardian of Islam's two holiest sites, Mecca and Medina, and uses this religious authority . Saudi Arabia's legal system is based on Sharia law, particularly as interpreted through the lens of Wahhabism. This has led to a very conservative legal framework that governs many aspects of life, from family law and gender roles to criminal justice.

Other Gulf countries also integrate Islam into their political systems, though to varying degrees. In Gulf countries , Islam is recognized as the state religion . Religious laws play a role in areas like family law, but some states legal systems also incorporates civil law,

The UAE thus presents a more modern, cosmopolitan approach to governance. While Islam is the official religion and Sharia plays a role in certain aspects of the legal system (particularly family law), the country also has a civil legal system, and its rulers have prioritized economic development, modernization, and international diplomacy over strict religious governance. However, the UAE still enforces conservative Islamic norms in areas like public morality and family law . In the UAE, modernization has been embraced in a way that allows for a balance between traditional religious values , to achieve a globalized economy , opening up the country to entertainment and tourism . The UAE's leadership has promoted a tolerant version of Islam and has sought to position the country as a hub for interfaith dialogue. While many in the Gulf support modernization, others view it as a threat to the religious and cultural fabric of the region.

As Gulf countries pursue modernization, they must navigate the fine balance between religious tradition and the demands of a modern economy and society. Reforms aimed at reducing the influence of conservative life have been met with resistance in some quarters.

The Gulf is home to growing expatriate populations from non-Muslim backgrounds, particularly in the UAE and Qatar. Managing the interfaith relations and ensuring religious freedom for these communities while maintaining Islamic identity is an ongoing challenge for Gulf governments. Almost all Gulf States have permitted construction of Christian and Catholic places of worship . UAE , Bahrain and Oman have each permitted Hindu temple on their land , while other religions have been given the option to practice their faith in private .

While the region is undergoing significant transformations, Islam continues to provide a foundation for both governance and personal life, even as its role is being renegotiated in the face of modernity and globalization. The future of the Gulf will likely be shaped by how these societies balance their Islamic heritage with the demands of the modern world.

CHAPTER 7

TRANSPORTATION

This chapter is all about getting around in the Gulf.

Transportation infrastructure in the Gulf region, has seen significant development over the past few decades. This growth is largely driven by the rapid urbanization, economic diversification, and the strategic importance of the Gulf states as global trade and tourism hubs. Here are some key points you can observe about the transportation infrastructure in the region once you relocate for work or otherwise to the Gulf States.

Road Networks that are designed mainly as Highway Systems . Gulf countries have invested heavily in modern highway systems to connect major cities and industrial hubs. For instance, Saudi Arabia has an extensive network of highways, such as the Riyadh–Dammam Highway, which connects key economic regions. Similarly, the UAE has well-developed roads like Sheikh Zayed Road, connecting Dubai and Abu Dhabi. Bahrain has the interstate highway , Bahrain Saudi causeway .

Multi-lane Highways and Ring roads are the highlight in this region . Many highways in the Gulf are multi-lane, well-maintained, and designed for high-speed traffic, with abundant speed cameras , which are in some cases monitored by AI technology . This reflects the need to accommodate both urban commuters and heavy-duty vehicles for industrial transport.

For layman expats living in Gulf countries, transportation options are varied depending on the country and the city, but in general, there are accessible and affordable means of getting around. Here's the most common options available

Public buses are one of the cheapest and most widely used modes of transport for expats, in all Guif Stares , especially those with limited incomes. These buses run regularly and connect different parts of cities and even rural areas.

Countries like the UAE (particularly Dubai and Abu Dhabi), Qatar, and Oman have well-developed public bus networks. In Dubai, for example, the Roads and Transport Authority (RTA) operates a large number of buses with good coverage across the city and they are reliable and safe . While affordable, bus services can be crowded during peak hours, and in some places, the waiting times can be long due to traffic congestion or less frequent routes in remote areas.

Cities like Dubai, Riyadh, and Doha have metro systems that are convenient for traveling within the urban core. The Dubai Metro is fully automated, clean, and has routes connecting major commercial and residential areas. Similarly, the Doha Metro has become a key mode of transport for residents. Metro fares are also reasonably priced and designed to be accessible for daily commuters. Metro systems are punctual, air-conditioned, and significantly faster than buses or cars in high-traffic areas. Metro networks though , are often limited to major cities, so if expats live in smaller towns or suburban areas, buses or taxis are more practical.

Taxis and ride hailing are widely available in most Gulf cities. They are a common choice for expats who prefer flexibility and convenience. Services like Uber and Careem (a popular local one , are widely available in cities such as Dubai, Riyadh, Doha, and Manama. These apps offer reliable stransport options with set fares, so you won't need to haggle over the price. While more expensive than public transport, taxis and ride-hailing services are reasonably priced, especially for short trips. Regular taxi usage can add up in cost, especially for longer distances. Also, during peak hours, finding a ride can be difficult, and surge pricing may apply for ride-hailing services.

Many expats, especially those in middle-income jobs, opt for informal carpooling or ride-sharing arrangements with colleagues or friends to save on transport costs. Some companies also arrange transportation for employees. But this is not always the case . In some Gulf countries, like Saudi Arabia and the UAE, private van or minibus services are popular among labor workers and lower-income expats. These services often have set routes and fixed rates. This is one of the cheapest options for expats who need to commute regularly but don't have access to a car.

Many expats, particularly those living in Gulf countries long-term, opt to buy or lease a car. Car prices are relatively affordable, and fuel is cheap in most Gulf countries due to government subsidies. To drive in the Gulf, expats usually need a valid local driving license. In some countries, you can convert your foreign license to a local one (depending on the nationality), but others may require a driving test.While purchasing a car is an upfront investment, owning one can offer more freedom and flexibility, especially for families or those living outside major urban areas . Driving in some Gulf countries can be very challenging due to heavy traffic, in peak hours , long distances, and aggressive driving habits.

Due to the extremely hot climate for most of the year, walking and cycling are not commonly used for long distances. However, in cooler months, some areas of cities like Dubai and Doha have pedestrian-friendly zones, parks, and cycling tracks. While not common for daily commuting, some cities have started promoting cycling as part of fitness and recreation programs, with dedicated cycle tracks being built in places like Dubai (e.g., the Nad Al Sheba and Al Qudra cycling tracks).

Many companies, particularly those in construction, hospitality, and other labor-intensive industries, provide transportation for their employees. This could include company buses that pick up and drop off workers at specific locations. This is usually free or included as part of the employment package and can be a reliable option for expats who work in specific industries . It can be less flexible, as it operates on fixed schedules and routes.

Car rental services are readily available for short-term needs. For example, expats who don't own cars often rent them on weekends or for travel between cities.In places like Dubai, water taxis (abras) are available for commuting across waterways, particularly the Dubai Creek area. These can be a scenic and affordable option for short distances

For layman expats, moving around Gulf countries is relatively easy with the various transport options available. Public buses and metro systems offer the most affordable solutions for daily commuting, while taxis and ride-hailing services provide more convenience. Car ownership is popular but not necessary for everyone, especially in cities with good public transportation infrastructure.

Given the economic integration within the Gulf Cooperation Council (GCC) countries, cross-border road networks are crucial. For instance, the King Fahd Causeway connects Saudi Arabia to Bahrain, facilitating trade and passenger movement.

GCC Railway Network is of the region's major proposed projects . This railway network, once completed which aims to connect all the member states with a 2,177 km railway. While the project has faced delays, it is seen as a key future component for boosting trade and reducing the region's reliance on road transport.

Some Gulf countries have already made progress in local rail networks. The UAE's Etihad Rail network aims to link all the emirates and provide an efficient cargo transport system. Similarly, Qatar's railway system, including the Doha Metro, supports urban mobility and World Cup-related infrastructure.

Light Rail and Metro Systems in the category of Urban metro systems have been introduced in cities like Dubai (Dubai Metro), Riyadh (Riyadh Metro, still under development), and Doha (Doha Metro), providing an efficient public transport alternative in rapidly growing urban environments.

The Gulf region's strategic location, particularly near the Strait of Hormuz, makes its ports vital for global maritime trade, especially in the oil and gas industries.Major ports such as Jebel Ali Port (UAE), King Abdul Aziz Port (Saudi Arabia), and Hamad Port (Qatar) are some of the largest and most technologically advanced in the world, handling millions of tons of cargo annually. Many ports in the Gulf have undergone significant expansions and upgrades to increase capacity and handle larger ships, particularly in response to increasing global trade demands and diversification strategies.

Gulf countries have become major players in the global aviation industry, and have recently become International hubs with large, modern airports like Dubai International (DXB), Hamad International (Doha), and King Khalid International (Riyadh). These airports are hubs for major airlines such as Emirates, Qatar Airways, and Etihad Airways, positioning the region as a key link between East and West. Many airports in the Gulf are continuously expanding to accommodate growing passenger and cargo traffic. Dubai International Airport, for example, is one of the busiest in the world for international passengers.

Bridges and Causeways like the King Fahd Causeway is a major infrastructure that links Saudi Arabia and Bahrain, facilitating both trade and tourism between the two countries. There are ongoing discussions about expanding or building additional causeways to further ease congestion. There have been proposals to build additional causeways linking Qatar to neighboring countries, as well as improving road links to accommodate the growing volume of trade and traffic in the region.

Despite the advanced infrastructure, the extreme climate conditions in the Gulf, particularly high temperatures, can make road maintenance challenging. Additionally, managing the rapid increase in vehicle ownership and traffic congestion in urban centers remains a concern.

Gulf countries are exploring more sustainable transportation solutions, such as electric vehicles and green public transport, to mitigate the environmental impact of traditional road and air transport. As Gulf cities continue to grow, there is increasing investment in smart city projects. These projects incorporate intelligent transportation systems (ITS) to manage traffic flow, reduce congestion, and enhance overall mobility.

Some Gulf countries, particularly the UAE, have shown interest in autonomous vehicles as part of their future urban transportation planning. Countries like Saudi Arabia and the UAE are investing in green infrastructure and public transportation systems to reduce carbon emissions, aligning with their broader sustainability goals, such as Saudi Arabia's Vision 2030 and the UAE's Net Zero by 2050 initiative.

In summary, the Gulf region's transportation infrastructure is highly developed and continues to evolve, reflecting both the economic importance of the region and the ambitious national development strategies in place. The integration of modern technology and sustainable practices will play a key role in its future trajectory.

CHAPTER 8

RECREATION FACILITIES

This chapter will cover the types of recreational activities, popular destinations, outdoor and indoor pursuits, and cultural and social aspects to help expatriates make the most of their stay in the Gulf region.

Recreational Activities for Expats in the Gulf Countries are numerous , provided one has the time and resources for it . The Gulf region has a unique combination of rich cultural heritage and modern infrastructure, making it an attractive place for expatriates from all over the world. With a warm climate seven months a year , diverse communities, and various leisure facilities, the GCC countries offer numerous recreational activities catering to different interests. From outdoor adventures to cultural experiences, expatriates can explore a wide range of recreational options suited for all age groups. Given the Gulf's generally warm weather, outside of the summer months , outdoor activities are popular, especially during the cooler months (October to April).

Desert Adventures like Dune Bashing are very popular in the Gulf .This thrilling activity is available across the UAE, Saudi Arabia, and Qatar. Experienced drivers take participants on an adrenaline-pumping ride over sand dunes in 4x4 vehicles.There are whole tourist packages in the UAE centering around Dune Bashing in the desert .

Camel Riding the next one , is an iconic Gulf experience, camel riding tours are offered in desert resorts and camps across the region, such as the Dubai Desert Conservation Reserve in the UAE or the Red Sands near Riyadh, Saudi Arabia.

Desert camping is popular among expats who want to experience a night under the stars. Various companies offer guided camping trips with traditional food, entertainment, and even stargazing.

With beautiful coastlines along the Persian Gulf and the Arabian Sea, beach activities and water sports are abundant. Popular beaches include Jumeirah Beach in Dubai, the Corniche in Abu Dhabi, Katara Beach in Qatar, and Marina Beach in Kuwait.

Water Sports options include jet skiing, kayaking, windsurfing, and parasailing, especially in the UAE and Oman. Snorkeling and diving are also available in the waters around Oman's Musandam Peninsula, known for its marine biodiversity.

The Gulf's clear waters and scenic coastline make it ideal for sailing and yachting. Many coastal cities offer yacht rentals and cruises, including Doha, Dubai, and Muscat.

While the Gulf is primarily known for its desert, some areas offer excellent hiking and trekking . For example, the Hajar Mountains in Oman and the UAE provide scenic trails like the Wadi Shab and Jebel Hafeet. Hiking enthusiasts can explore nature reserves like the Al Wathba Wetland Reserve in Abu Dhabi or the Ras Al Khor Wildlife Sanctuary in Dubai.

The Gulf's hot summers make indoor recreation appealing, and the region has developed many facilities catering to indoor pursuits. Shopping Malls and Entertainment Centers are dotted throughout the Gulf . Shopping is a popular activity in the Gulf, and malls are often multi-functional spaces. They feature high-end stores, dining options, entertainment centers, cinemas, and sometimes theme parks. Notable malls include Dubai Mall (UAE), Emirates Mall (UAE) , Villaggio Mall (Qatar), and Avenues Mall (Kuwait).

Dubai however , offers some of the world's largest indoor theme parks, such as IMG Worlds of Adventure and the Aquarium . Other

Gulf countries too have entertainment zones within malls, including KidZania and VR parks.

Most GCC countries have modern gyms and sports centers with facilities for squash, badminton, and tennis. Expats can also enjoy bowling, laser tag, paint ball and arcade gaming in venues like Bounce (trampoline parks) in Dubai, Riyadh, and Doha.

Ski Dubai in the Mall of the Emirates provides a unique indoor skiing experience in a country without natural snow. Indoor climbing walls and skate parks are also available.

Regarding Cultural and Artistic Pursuits , there are several Museums and Art Galleries in all Gulf States . Expats interested in art and history can explore institutions like the Louvre Abu Dhabi, the Museum of Islamic Art in Doha, and the Bahrain National Museum. Many galleries host exhibitions featuring both local and international artists.

Community centers and private organizations offer classes and workshops in pottery, painting, and photography, often organized by expat communities or cultural centers. This can be a great way to meet other expats and locals.

Community centers and social clubs play a significant role in recreational life for expats, offering social and cultural engagement by various activities . Many cities have expat clubs that cater to various nationalities, such as British Clubs, American Societies, and Indian Associations, which organize social gatherings, sporting events, and cultural festivals.

Amateur sports leagues in cities like Dubai, Riyadh, and Doha offer soccer, rugby, and cricket teams that expats can join, providing a way to stay active and make friends.

Expats can join language and cultural exchange meetups, which are popular in cities with diverse communities like Dubai and Doha. These groups allow participants to practice languages and learn about other cultures.

Expatriates with an interest in culinary arts can attend cooking classes and food festivals , especially in the UAE, Bahrain, and Qatar. Seasonal food festivals like the Dubai Food Festival showcase international and local cuisine.

For those seeking relaxation and wellness activities, the Gulf has a variety of options. Almost every GCC country boasts luxury spas and Wellness Centers , offering massages, beauty treatments, and wellness therapies. Renowned hotel spas include the Talise Spa in Dubai and Anantara Spa in Oman

Yoga studios and Meditation retreats are popular in cities like Muscat, Dubai, and Doha. Retreats are often held in scenic locations, such as the desert or by the beach, providing a peaceful environment.

Golf is a favored recreational activity in the Gulf, albeit mostly for the upper income ,classes with many world-class golf courses. Notable courses include the Emirates Golf Club in Dubai, the Doha Golf Club, and the Muscat Hills Golf & Country Club.

Experiencing local festivals and cultural events allows all expatriates to connect with the Gulf region's heritage and traditions. Partaking in the host countries National Day Celebrations offers a festive feel .Each GCC country celebrates its national day with large-scale events, parades, fireworks, and cultural performances, such as UAE National Day , and Saudi National Day. All expats are welcome to participate in these public festivities and it's seen that they do it wholeheartedly.

Islamic holidays like Eid al-Fitr and Eid al-Adha are significant celebrations with week long holidays , public events, special meals, charities and cultural activities. Expatriates can witness traditional hospitality and cultural customs during these times. Remember to be always respectful of the traditions of your host country .

Events like the Al Janadriyah Festival in Saudi Arabia and Muscat Festival in Oman celebrate traditional music, dance, and art, offering a rich cultural experience for expats.

Adventure , Road Trips and Day Trips are very popular in the Gulf States . Many expats enjoy exploring nearby destinations for a quick getaway. Road trips to scenic spots such as the mountains of Oman, the beaches of Fujairah, or the dunes of Liwa Oasis in Abu Dhabi are popular. Expats with a car can enjoy weekend excursions , and discover remote scenic areas in the host country with spectacular views.

The GCC's proximity to multiple countries allows for short international trips to neighboring countries. Expatriates can travel easily between the Gulf countries or visit nearby destinations like Jordan, Egypt, or even the Maldives for a weekend break.

Recreational opportunities for expatriates in the Gulf are thus diverse and reflect the region's mix of tradition and modernity. From exploring the natural beauty of deserts and beaches to experiencing the thrill of water sports, cultural festivals, and fine dining, the Gulf countries provide a wide array of activities that make life enjoyable for expats. By engaging in these recreational activities, expatriates can build connections, gain a deeper understanding of Gulf culture, and create lasting memories during their stay in this unique region. Gulf offers something for everyone, fostering an environment where expatriates can thrive and engage in fulfilling leisure pursuits.

CHAPTER 9

WORLD CLASS SHOPPING

The Gulf offers a Glittering Shopping Experience. All Gulf states are Global Retail Destinations in terms of goods imports . The Gulf region, particularly cities like Dubai, Abu Dhabi, Doha, and Riyadh, has transformed into a shopping haven over recent decades. Known for their architectural marvels, extravagant shopping festivals, and tax-free prices, Gulf shopping centers offer an experience that merges luxury and affordability, attracting millions of tourists and residents alike. From the sleek malls of Dubai to traditional souks of Bahrain, the Gulf is where East meets West, creating a unique blend of cultural richness and modern retail dynamism.

The retail landscape in the Gulf grew alongside economic diversification, with leaders investing oil revenue to transform these regions into international business and tourism hubs. Beginning in the 1980s, global luxury brands entered cities like Dubai, setting the foundation for the Gulf's luxurious shopping reputation. As oil wealth fueled rapid urbanization, retail infrastructure expanded at an unprecedented rate, transforming cities into cosmopolitan centers where international brands, high-tech malls, and multicultural consumer bases coexist.

Key Milestones in UAE are listed here . In 1983 , The BurJuman Centre in Dubai becomes one of the first upscale malls, attracting luxury brands and setting a precedent for future developments of the Gulf region .

1996: Dubai launches the Dubai Shopping Festival, a month-long event that grows into one of the region's biggest attractions today for tourists seeking exclusive discounts, tax-free shopping, and entertainment.

2005: The opening of the Mall of the Emirates, complete with an indoor ski resort, marks the UAE's position as a global retail powerhouse.

These are just the notable examples .Each Gulf city boasts unique iconic Malls , attractive shopping environments, designed to cater to a range of consumer experiences, from high-end luxury boutiques to family-friendly attractions. Malls are not just shopping venues but destinations that feature dining, food courts , entertainment, and cultural exhibits, presenting a full-day experience that transcends traditional retail.

Dubai is currently The Pinnacle of Luxury and Innovation . Dubai malls are architectural and experiential masterpieces, offering everything from aquariums to VR amusement parks. The Dubai Mall , known as the largest mall in the world by total area, it offers over 1,200 stores, including flagship luxury stores from brands like Gucci, Chanel, and Rolex. Attractions like the Dubai Aquarium, an Olympic-sized ice rink, and the Burj Khalifa's direct access , add to its allure.

Mall of the Emirates is home to Ski Dubai, the Middle East's first indoor ski slope, it's a prime attraction for those seeking both luxury and novelty. Luxury brands, fine dining, and cultural events make it a must-visit for tourists and locals.

Doha however prefers fusing Tradition with Modernity . Qatar's capital presents a sophisticated shopping experience blending contemporary luxury with local heritage. Villaggio Mall which was styled after Venetian canals, the design transports shoppers to a European setting while hosting luxury brands like Valentino and Louis Vuitton. Souq Waqif , although not a modern mall, this traditional market is an integral part of the Gulf shopping experience. Here, visitors find authentic Qatari crafts, spices, perfumes, and an atmosphere that celebrates the rich heritage of the region.

With its growing population and rapid modernization, Saudi Arabia's retail sector has surged too into an emerging shopping hub . The Kingdom Centre Mall , located within Riyadh's Kingdom Tower, caters to high-end consumers and offers an elevated luxury experience, with international brands and high-quality services. The Riyadh Park Mall known for its family-friendly amenities and entertainment, this mall emphasizes Saudi Arabia's commitment to blending retail with recreation, catering to both local and expatriate families.

The Blend of cultural Souks and Modern Marketplaces is seen everywhere in the Gulf . While the Gulf region boasts world-class malls, it also cherishes till today , its traditional markets, known as "souks," which offer an immersive cultural experience. These souks provide a counterpoint to the modern mall scene, allowing tourists and residents to engage with local crafts, perfumes, and artisan products.

One of the most famous souks in the world, the Gold Souk in Deira offers gold jewelry at competitive prices. Buyers are encouraged to haggle, and the souk's vast selection includes intricate designs reflecting Arabian, Indian, and international styles.

Muttrah Souk, Oman is a traditional market in Muscat providing a charming glimpse into Omani culture. Its narrow alleyways are lined with shops selling frankincense, textiles, and handicrafts unique to Oman.

Souq Al Mubarakiyya, Kuwait is one of the oldest souks in Kuwait City, Al Mubarakiyya offers an range of goods, from spices and dates to carpets and jewelry, making it a very popular spot for both locals and tourists.

The Shopping Festival Extravaganza in the Gulf are significant events that draw millions of international visitors every year. These festivals highlight the region's retail clout and allow shoppers to find exclusive deals and participate in special events.

The most notable is the Dubai Shopping Festival (DSF) . Launched in 1996, DSF has become one of the Gulf's largest shopping and entertainment events, attracting over five million visitors annually. Held every winter, it offers discounts across Dubai's malls, accompanied by concerts, raffles, and family-friendly activities. DSF's unique combination of retail and entertainment has elevated Dubai's reputation as a top destination for shopping tourism.

Abu Dhabi Shopping Festival comes next . Abu Dhabi's retail landscape has grown in recent years, with the Abu Dhabi Shopping Festival emerging as an event that celebrates the city's burgeoning luxury scene. Featuring exclusive brand collaborations, designer showcases, and international cuisine, this festival is a testament to Abu Dhabi's rise as a retail hub.

Qatar Shopping Festival hosted by Doha hosts an annual shopping festival with discounts, promotions, and luxury brand showcases. Like DSF, this festival also includes cultural and family events, positioning Qatar as a rising shopping destination in the Gulf.

It's notable that the Gulf region attracts nearly every major multinational brand across fashion, technology, home goods, and cuisine. However, what makes the Gulf's retail sector distinct is how these global brands adapt to meet local preferences and local influences

Fashion and Luxury brands often offer exclusive collections for the Gulf, including modest wear to suit cultural tastes. Gucci, Dior, and Burberry have all created capsule collections for Gulf consumers, featuring traditional silhouettes and color palettes. Scent is a very significant part of Gulf culture, and brands like Chanel and Jo Malone have created oud-inspired fragrances specifically for the Middle Eastern market. IKEA, West Elm, and Pottery Barn all maintain a robust presence in the region, adapting their inventories to reflect the Gulf's emphasis on luxury and contemporary decor.

For residents and visitors alike, shopping in the Gulf is often a full-day affair, where one can move seamlessly from high-end stores to theme parks and gourmet dining, all under one roof.

The Gulf's retail landscape embodies a synergy of tradition and modernity, of luxury and accessibility. For travelers and residents, the Gulf offers a unique shopping experience unparalleled in scale and diversity. Malls are not merely venues for commerce but cultural centers, allowing visitors to experience the Gulf's identity in all its splendor. With malls that rival the size of small cities and souks that capture centuries-old trade practices, shopping in the Gulf is a journey that combines commerce, culture, and community into one unforgettable experience.

CHAPTER 10

CLIMATE

Climate Challenges in the Gulf Region and an overview climate characteristics are dealt in this chapter . The Gulf region experiences extreme temperatures, arid landscapes, and limited freshwater resources. Seasonal variability includes intense summer heat and mild to moderate winters, punctuated by seasonal dust storms and occasional seasonal winter rain.

The Gulf lies in an area with limited rainfall, and geographical vulnerability, high salinity in coastal waters, and ecosystems adapted to desert and marine life . Rising sea levels threaten low-lying coastal cities and islands.

Rising Temperatures and Heatwaves are the normal scenario in the Gulf . Intensity and Duration of Temperatures frequently exceed 50°C (122°F) in summer, affecting human health, infrastructure, and energy demands. Impacts are also felt on Labor Productivity . Outdoor workers, especially in construction and oil sectors, face heightened risk of heat stress, limiting safe working hours. Increased demand for air conditioning leads to greater electricity consumption, increasing reliance on fossil fuels. In hottest summer hours outdoor works are prohibited by the authorities in the Gulf .

Public Health Concerns in the Gulf are to a large extent health risks , that include heat exhaustion, heat stroke, and dehydration, disproportionately affecting vulnerable populations. Hospitals face strain due to heat-related illnesses in the scorching summer especially in densely populated urban areas.

The Gulf region has one of the lowest levels of natural freshwater availability per capita in the world. Limited groundwater and minimal rainfall necessitate heavy reliance on desalination. Energy-intensive desalination processes pose a challenge by increasing carbon emissions, despite providing essential water resources. The brine discharge from desalination plants raises salinity in the Persian Gulf, impacting marine biodiversity and ecosystems.

Future Demand Projections due to population growth and urbanization increase water demand, creating pressure to expand desalination despite environmental impacts. Rising sea levels may threaten ports, airports, and urban centers in coastal cities like Dubai, Abu Dhabi, and Doha . The sea level rise could erode the coastline posing a threat to coastal infrastructure . Infrastructure such as roads, bridges, and oil facilities may require extensive adaptation or relocation.

Frequent salinization could affect inland areas, contaminating groundwater and soils with saltwater. Marine Ecosystem Degradation and Coastal ecosystems, including mangroves and coral reefs, face risk of degradation, due to this phenomenon, impacting fisheries and biodiversity.

Increased Frequency of Dust Storms and subsequent rising temperatures and aridity lead to air quality degradation and soil degradation, making dust storms more frequent and severe. Impacts on Human health by dust particles can exacerbate respiratory diseases, including asthma and bronchitis, posing severe risks to public health . Dust storms frequently lead to poor visibility and disruptions in traffic . Dust storms reduce visibility, leading to accidents and sometimes disruption in air and ground transportation.

Economic Implications of this is the frequent clean-up operations and maintenance of machinery, buildings, and infrastructure . This increases operational costs for businesses. Impacts on Terrestrial Biodiversity and ecosystem stress by extreme temperatures and water scarcity reduce the resilience of native plant and animal species. Urban expansion and desertification threaten remaining natural habitats, particularly for unique desert flora and fauna.

Marine biodiversity Concerns are also present in the Gulf region . Rising sea temperatures and increased salinity due to desalination impact coral reefs, a vital ecosystem for fish populations. Decline in marine biodiversity gradually affects local fisheries and food security. Surprisingly , even though most of Gulf has access to coastline , all types of seafood are a pricier commodities in the gulf

Economic and Social Vulnerabilities of the climate conditions have an Impact on Oil and Gas Sector . Extreme heat usually affects the productivity and safety of oil and gas operations, a key economic driver in the Gulf. The cost of cooling facilities and maintaining safe working conditions rises correspondingly as temperatures increase. Energy and Water Demand for Growing populations and urbanization increase demand for both water and energy, leading to potential shortages or energy shortages .

Climate-induced impacts could force relocations, particularly in low-lying coastal areas or regions affected by extreme heat. Internal migration toward cities may increase, creating additional pressure on urban infrastructure and services.

Adaptation Strategies are being followed and regional collaboration is sought . Energy Transition and Renewable Investments are now serious topics pursued in the Gulf . The Gulf Cooperation Council (GCC) countries are investing in solar energy to reduce carbon emissions and reliance on fossil fuels. Strategies include renewable energy initiatives, like the construction of large solar plants in the UAE and Saudi Arabia.

Water Management Innovations are ongoing in several Gulf States . Countries are exploring water conservation, rainwater harvesting, and advanced desalination technologies. Investments in recycled and get water systems help reduce pressure on freshwater resources.

Urban Planning and Infrastructure Adaptation are actively being implemented . Coastal defenses, green infrastructure, and heat-resistant building materials are being developed for climate resilience. Smart cities initiatives aim to integrate climate adaptation into urban planning, enhancing sustainability. The GCC countries are collaborating on shared regional policies, including early warning systems and climate monitoring networks.

In the path forward , The Gulf region faces a challenging road ahead as it adapts to escalating climate risks. Innovative technology, regional cooperation, and robust policy initiatives will be critical in mitigating the impacts of climate change on economies, health, and biodiversity. While climate adaptation requires significant investment, it offers opportunities for sustainable growth and leadership in green technologies in the region .

This chapter provided a structured overview of the current climate-related challenges faced by expats and locals the Gulf region, from a layman point of view , emphasizing both current issues and forward-looking solutions for resilience.

CHAPTER 11

CUISINES OF THE GULF

A detailed chapter on Gulf State cuisines exploring the culinary landscape across the Gulf nations, revealing how traditional flavors have evolved alongside modern eating trends. The tastes of the Gulf are a delightful mix of traditions and

innovation . Gulf State Cuisines and Culinary Culture follow a melting pot of flavors .

Gulf's cuisine, is mostly historical . touching on influences from Persia, India, Africa, and the Mediterranean. The ancient trade routes brought with them spices, ingredients, and techniques that still flavor today's Gulf cuisine. It's currently a blend of local heritage with global tastes. Staples and signature ingredients are dates, rice, Arabic Pita bread , fish, lamb, saffron, and spices such as cardamom, turmeric, and cinnamon.

Dates hold great importance in the Gulf society , as both a dietary staple and a symbol of hospitality. It's also extensively grown in all Gulf States and is featured prominently in Ramadan season . One can Explore the great variety of seafood caught fresh from the waters of the Gulf . Fresh grilled fish and dried fish are coastal staples. Each Gulf country uses seafood uniquely.

Classic Dishes with a taste of heritage include Majboos , A spiced rice and meat dish, often considered the national dish and continuing favorite across the Gulf.Other Favorites include Harees, A porridge-like dish made with wheat and meat, enjoyed especially during Ramadan , Thareed A bread stew dish, often featuring vegetables and meat, popular during special occasions , Saloona , A hearty stew made with vegetables, meat, and spices, served often with rice or bread. And Balaleet , A sweet and savory breakfast dish with vermicelli and egg.

In addition , different Gulf States add their unique touches to common dishes. Thus Kuwait's love for fried fish and distinct use of saffron. Saudi Arabia's Kabsa with its own delightful spice blend. Oman's Shuwa, a slow-cooked, marinated meat dish prepared in underground sand pits. Bahrain's emphasis though is on sweet and spicy combinations, especially in their seafood dishes.

The culinary influences are from nearby regions like Persia, India, and East Africa. Indian spices are widely used and also the subcontinent s cooking techniques, especially evident in biryanis and curries. The influence of Persia is evident in grilled meats and bread. African influence , minimally seen in the use of dried fish and coconut in coastal Gulf cuisine.

Modern Dining and Fusion Food trends however is widely favored in the Gulf States Gulf's vibrant cities have transformed into international culinary hubs . High-end restaurants and international fusion cuisine are seen in cities like Dubai, Doha, and Riyadh. The popularity of global food trends such as sushi, gourmet burgers are immense , and fusion concepts that blend Gulf flavors with international dishes are seen widely practiced . The rise of celebrity chefs in high end establishments in the Gulf States is now a trend .

Immensely popular with all levels of society , are Street Cafes, Street Food, and Casual Dining. There are multitudes of popular street food and cafes, where locals , expats and tourists alike enjoy more relaxed dining. Shawarma stands and falafel stalls are also favored as a quick and popular choice across Gulf cities. In Traditional coffee houses Arabic coffee (gahwa) and tea are served with dates.The modern cafes serve specialty coffee, artisan pastries, and creative twists on local flavors (e.g., saffron-infused cakes or cardamom-spiced desserts).

Food is a cultural expression in Gulf cultural and religious celebrations .Traditional meals during Ramadan and Eid, including special Iftar and Suhoor dishes are a staple throughout the Gulf States . Wedding feasts with elaborate platters of meat and rice, called Ouzi are the norm , together with dozens of local Gulf delicacies , all plentifully served and shared , reflecting the Gulf family's hospitality. National Day feasts, also showcase these classic dishes unique to each Gulf nation. As winter begins , locals and expats are seen heading to the desert camps and chalets for some chilling out and cook over traditional open fire grills .

Expat dining scene in the Gulf States thus is a matter of choosing from the multitudes of cuisines available . From street cafes and restaurants selling simple grills and rotisserie , sandwiches , shawarmas , vegetarian dips like hommous and a variety of Indian flatbreads and curries , not to mention dozens Chinese food options , the list is endless . Gulf States have food varieties to suit everyone . Some Gulf States have subsidized a few daily staples to enable the common man to not lack anything. This includes Arabian Pita style bread , Kubz , which is also a staple all over the Gulf States and is also very popular with all categories of expats and locals .

Lately however there is a rising trend in the Gulf States , towards Sustainable and Farm-to-Table Dining . Produce is sourced locally reflecting recent trends in sustainability, and farm-to-table restaurants across the Gulf .

Gulf governments have taken the idea of growing vegetables and certain fruits including dates , very seriously through desert farming and aquaculture . All steps are being done to provide irrigation to the local farms , support to market these local grown products and this is now reshaping food production in the region.

The aim is to cut dependence from imports of produce by at least a third .

Most popular restaurants are patrons of local home grown and organic produce . The industry is thus thriving . There are several farms in the Gulf States producing a sizable output of produce , poultry and eggs , cheese and farm milk which is delivered daily to the groceries and even to households . This growing interest in plant-based and health-conscious eating, reflecting global shifts .

Gulf's commitment to honoring its roots while embracing the diversity of its modern dining scene is reflected in the culinary habits . Gulf States' cuisine is a celebration and a testament to the region's resilience, hospitality, and vibrant, evolving culture.Gulf cuisines , are rich with history, flavor, and the warmth of tradition, yet ever-evolving in its global dining landscape. An expat who has lived and worked in the Gulf States will never ever forget the tastes of Arabian food .

CHAPTER 12

DRESS CODES

Understanding Dress Codes and Cultural Norms in the Gulf Region takes a bit of effort and understanding. The Gulf region is known for its rich cultural heritage, conservative values, and adherence to Islamic traditions. For expatriates relocating to Gulf countries , understanding and respecting local dress codes is essential to integrating into society smoothly and respectfully. This chapter delves into the general dress norms, guidelines, and tips for adapting to these expectations in different scenarios, such as in public, work environments, and social gatherings.

Understanding the Cultural Context is crucial when following Gulf dress codes . The Gulf countries are governed by Islamic principles, which strongly influence cultural norms, including dress codes. While the level of strictness may vary by country, most Gulf nations expect people to dress modestly as a sign of respect for local customs and traditions. Wearing modest clothing that covers the shoulders, arms, and knees is typically appreciated and expected.

Additionally, these expectations often extend to expatriates as well, particularly in government buildings, religious sites, and traditional neighborhoods. Adhering to these dress codes demonstrates cultural sensitivity and respect, which can enhance relationships and ease the transition for newcomers.

General Dress Code Guidelines are influenced by modesty. Modesty is the keyword. Both men and women are encouraged to dress conservatively in public areas. Clothing should not be overly tight, revealing, nor transparent. In most Gulf countries, it is common for men and women to wear clothing that covers their shoulders and knees. This applies in public spaces such as malls, parks, and restaurants. Clothing with offensive images, slogans, or politically sensitive messages should be avoided. In professional settings, especially in sectors like finance or government, formal and conservative clothing is often the standard.

Guidelines for Women dress codes in public spaces .In most Gulf countries, women are expected to dress modestly. Wearing long skirts, dresses, or loose trousers with tops that cover the shoulders is advised. Abayas and Headscarves are worn extensively in the Gulf region . In Saudi Arabia, wearing an abaya (a loose-fitting black cloak) is mandatory for all women, including expatriates, though a headscarf may be optional in many parts. In the UAE, Qatar, and Bahrain, expatriate women are not required to wear an abaya but may choose to do so in more traditional or religious settings. When visiting mosques or other religious sites, women should wear an abaya and cover their hair with a headscarf. Long sleeves and long skirts or pants are also recommended to show respect.

Modest swimwear is expected in public beaches and hotel pools, and one-piece suits or burkinis may be preferable. Bikinis are generally allowed in private beaches or specific resort areas.

Men are advised to wear trousers or long shorts that reach the knees, along with shirts that cover the shoulders in public spaces . Some expatriates may choose to wear the local dishdasha (long white robe) to blend in, though this is not mandatory. Wearing traditional attire should be done respectfully, and some may choose to seek local advice first. Long trousers and modest shirts are recommended when visiting religious sites. Short-sleeved shirts may be acceptable, but sleeveless tops are considered very inappropriate. On public beaches, men are expected to wear modest swim shorts. Swimming trunks or tight-fitting swimwear may be allowed only at private beach clubs or hotels.

Workplace Dress Codes for Corporate Sector are generally as follows .For men, a suit and tie may be required in corporate settings. Women should opt for dresses or skirts that fall below the knee and blouses with sleeves. Pantsuits are also a popular choice for women in business.

In government offices or meetings, dressing conservatively is often mandatory. Men may be required to wear long-sleeved shirts with ties, and women should dress professionally and modestly.

Some private companies, following business casual settings particularly those with a large expatriate workforce, may adopt a more relaxed dress code. However, even in such settings, covering shoulders and knees remains important.

Expatriates should make an effort to understand the nature of social gatherings, which can vary greatly in terms of formality. Formal events may call for more traditional or conservative dress, while informal gatherings might be more lenient. During events like weddings or religious celebrations, some expatriates choose to wear traditional attire as a sign of respect. This is generally welcomed, as long as the attire is worn properly and respectfully.

Due to the Gulf's extreme heat, finding a balance between modesty and comfort is key. Loose, breathable fabrics like cotton or linen are highly recommended. Most malls and stores in the Gulf offer clothing options that meet local expectations, including longer dresses, tunics, and kaftans. Shopping locally can be a way to find regionally appropriate clothing that aligns with cultural norms.

Exceptions and Variances are noticed from country to country . Dubai, in particular, is relatively liberal, and many dress codes are relaxed in tourist areas and malls. However, even in these areas, modest dress is still appreciated.

In Saudi Arabia Dress codes are stricter, especially for women. Wearing an abaya in public is mandatory, though in recent years, enforcement has eased in certain areas. The other countries in the region have moderate dress codes. While expatriates are not required to wear local attire, modest clothing is recommended, especially outside of expatriate-heavy areas. Known for its conservative culture,

Gulf States encourages expatriates to dress modestly, especially in rural areas and traditional markets. Places like mosques, government buildings, and traditional markets have stricter dress codes. Keeping a shawl or scarf handy can be helpful for women. Even casual gatherings may expect a level of modesty, particularly when attending events with local families. Erring on the side of conservative dressing is generally wise.

Certain religious observances, such as Ramadan, come with heightened expectations of modesty for everyone, including expatriates. Local women do not use make up during the fasting hours . Adhering to the dress codes in the Gulf region not only shows respect for local culture but also helps expatriates integrate more smoothly and avoid unnecessary confrontations. While the specifics may vary across the Gulf countries, the underlying principle of modesty remains a common thread. Embracing these dress norms, while keeping cultural sensitivities in mind, can help expatriates build positive relationships, foster respect, and thrive in their new environment.

CHAPTER 13

These certificates are often necessary for travel within the GCC (Gulf Cooperation Council) region.

Microchipping is mandatory in many Gulf states, as it aids in reuniting lost pets with their owners. Veterinarians and government agencies use databases to keep track of registered animals.

Certain animals are prohibited as pets across the Gulf states, often for reasons related to public health, safety, or environmental impact. Exotic animal ownership has been heavily regulated or banned in response to rising awareness about animal welfare and public safety concerns. In Gulf countries, residents cannot legally keep wild or exotic animals as pets. Examples of restricted species include Lions, tigers, cheetahs, and other big cats, all reptiles including snakes and crocodiles are often prohibited. Gulf countries also ban ownership of primates like monkeys, as they can pose a risk to humans .

In cases where residents wish to own exotic pets (such as specific bird species), they may need to apply for special permits from wildlife or environmental authorities. These permits ensure that the animals are legally sourced, cared for responsibly, and do not pose a threat to public safety. Many Gulf residents see pet ownership as a responsibility, with an emphasis on kindness and care.

Owning a pet in the Gulf region requires an understanding of unique climate challenges, legal regulations, and cultural nuances. With proper care, responsible ownership, and adherence to vaccination and health standards, pet owners in the Gulf can create a safe and loving environment for their animals, enhancing their own well-being and that of their pets.

CHAPTER 14

HORSES AND FALCONRY

Horses and Falconry is a Partnership in Nobility and Skill . Throughout history, horses and falconry have held a unique place in many cultures, symbolizing power, prestige, and skill. They were essential to hunting practices and became interwoven with traditions of nobility, war, and even sport. The relationship between horses and falconry represents a blend of loyalty, intuition, and mastery, as both horse and falcon handler must coordinate seamlessly to achieve their goals.

Horses have been instrumental in falconry for centuries, especially in cultures where vast landscapes required hunters to cover large distances. Mounted falconry allowed handlers to follow their falcons across plains and through forests with speed and efficiency. The bond between a horse and its rider was crucial; a calm, well-trained horse allowed the falconer to focus on their bird, confident that the horse would remain steady and responsive under challenging conditions.

The choice of horse in falconry was also significant. While endurance was a key factor, so was temperament. A steady horse was essential, as sudden movements or reactions could easily frighten a falcon and disrupt the delicate process of hunting. Breeds known for endurance and calm temperaments, such as Arabian and Barb horses, were often favored by falconers across the Middle East, where falconry has a long history.

Falconry seen as a Noble Pursuit in the Gulf regions . Falconry was often associated with nobility and prestige. In many parts of the world, it was a practice reserved for the elite. In medieval Europe, laws governed who could own and train falcons, with only the highest-ranking individuals allowed to fly certain species. For instance, only royalty could fly eagles, while falcons were typically reserved for lords and knights. This association with status and privilege was mirrored in the Middle East and Central Asia, where sultans and khans would often hunt with elaborate entourages, showcasing their wealth and skill.

The practice of falconry required time, patience, and resources. Training a falcon to hunt took months, even years, and falconers needed to devote themselves fully to the craft. The training process also required space and specific equipment, such as hoods, gloves, and perches, and a deep understanding of the falcon's behavior and instincts. Because of the complexity and expense, only the wealthy could afford to practice falconry, further cementing its status as a noble pursuit.

Training both horses and falcons for hunting required a delicate balance of discipline and empathy. For horses, training involved teaching them to respond to the falconer's subtle cues, such as shifting weight or slight tugs on the reins, as well as desensitizing them to the movements of the falcon overhead. Horses needed to stay calm and motionless when the falcon was released, as any sudden movement could disrupt the hunt.

The training of the falcon itself was even more complex. Falconers used food as the primary incentive in the Gulf , teaching the bird to associate specific signals, such as a whistle or hand motion, with the reward of food. This process, known as "manning," involved long hours of building trust and overcoming the falcon's natural wariness. Initially, falcons are trained to sit on the falconer's glove and accept small pieces of food. Gradually, they learn to fly short distances to the falconer and eventually to hunt game.

The relationship between falconer and bird is one of mutual respect rather than dominance. Unlike domesticated animals, birds of prey retain their wild instincts and cannot be forced to obey. Falconers must learn to read the bird's body language, understanding its moods and motivations. The success of the hunt depends on the falcon's willingness to return to the handler, a decision the bird makes voluntarily. This unique partnership highlights the bond of trust and respect that underpins falconry.

A typical hunt in the Gulf involving horses and falcons requires precision and coordination. The falconer rides out with the horse, scouting the landscape for potential prey. Once game, is spotted, the falconer releases the bird, which immediately takes flight, scanning the ground below. The falcon's keen eyesight and ability to fly at high speeds make it an effective hunter, capable of spotting and catching prey that a human or horse might miss.

The horse plays a critical role in this phase of the hunt as well. The falconer must follow the falcon's flight, keeping within range but not startling the prey. The horse needs to navigate the terrain skillfully, maintaining a steady pace and allowing the falconer to focus entirely on the bird. In this complex dance, horse and falconer work together to support the falcon, each playing their part in a timeless ritual of nature and skill.

In addition to its practical applications, the practice of falconry and mounted hunting carries a deep cultural significance in many regions. In the Middle East, falconry has long been a symbol of heritage and identity, and it remains a popular pastime, especially in countries like the United Arab Emirates and Saudi Arabia.

Falconry was often depicted in art and literature as an allegory for chivalry and nobility, emphasizing the virtues of the hunter who respects his quarry and partners. It's no wonder that falconry continues to capture the imagination, even in modern times, as a living connection to the natural world and our shared heritage.

The legacy of horses and falconry extends beyond practical hunting. Today, both are celebrated as cultural heritage, with festivals and competitions that honor the skills and traditions associated with the craft. Falconry has been recognized by UNESCO as an Intangible Cultural Heritage, and preservation efforts continue to protect this ancient art form. Similarly, horseback riding remains a treasured tradition, with numerous events and practices celebrating the special bond between human and horse.

Falconry and horses offer us a glimpse into a way of life that valued patience, partnership, and respect for the natural world. This legacy is alive and well in the communities that continue to practice these arts, and in the admiration that people around the world feel for the beauty and skill involved in the partnership between horse, falconer, and falcon. In a world where technology often distances us from nature, the art of falconry and horseback hunting remains a powerful reminder of the ancient, enduring bond between humans and animals.

CHAPTER 15

PREMIUM LUXURY VEHICLES AND OPULENCE

Vehicle Culture and Luxury in the Gulf States are dealt in this chapter . Gulf states are synonymous with opulence, modernity, and a high standard of living. Their vehicle culture reflects this lifestyle, with a focus on high-performance cars, luxury vehicles, and customized options. In these countries, owning a premium car is more than just about transportation; it's a symbol of social status, personal style, and an expression of a strong car culture rooted in the region's wealth and fascination with innovation. This chapter explores the unique car culture of the Gulf, the types of vehicles commonly chosen, and the luxurious, often personalized nature of these choices together with the layman's choices .

The Gulf's love affair with luxury cars can be traced back to the historical context, when oil was discovered in the mid-20th century, which catapulted the region's economies into high gear. With rapid modernization, residents in cities like Dubai, Abu Dhabi, and Riyadh gained disposable incomes that could be invested in luxurious and exotic cars. As Gulf countries became global trading hubs, access to high-end and niche vehicles increased, fueling a deep interest in automotive prestige. Today, the Gulf states rank among the world's most significant markets for luxury car brands, while major car shows and rallies reinforce this culture.

For many Gulf residents, particularly in the wealthy classes, high performance and luxury brands like Rolls-Royce, Bentley, Ferrari, Lamborghini, Bugatti, and Porsche are emblematic of social status and prestige . These vehicles are not only seen as symbols of wealth but also as indicators of taste and sophistication. Each brand is associated with specific values and traits.

Rolls-Royce and Bentley are known for their classic design, luxurious interiors, and attention to detail, these brands are popular among high-profile businessmen and government officials who appreciate both comfort and style. The customization options offered by Rolls-Royce, for instance, appeal to Gulf buyers, who often request unique colors, interiors, and added touches that reflect personal status.

Ferrari and Lamborghini are iconic Italian brands embody performance, speed, and flair. They are especially popular with younger buyers and car enthusiasts who crave adrenaline-pumping experiences. In cities like Dubai, these supercars are very common sights on the streets and in luxury car events, where owners can showcase their vehicles.

Bugatti is known for producing some of the most powerful and expensive vehicles in the world, Bugatti holds a special place in Gulf car culture. Owning a Bugatti is seen as the ultimate status symbol, as it represents both immense wealth and an appreciation for automotive engineering at the highest level.

Porsche and Mercedes-Benz , preferred in the Gulf for those who appreciate a blend of luxury and practicality, Porsche's SUVs and sports cars and Mercedes-Benz's high-end S-Class and AMG models offer a mix of performance, reliability, and high-end comfort. Mercedes-Benz Maybach models also cater to buyers in Gulf States seeking a more discreet form of opulence.

These brands , not surprisingly have created Gulf-exclusive models with unique color schemes and finishes, and they often customize their interiors to include symbols and features tied to local culture, such as Arabic calligraphy or sand-inspired color palettes.

Vehicle customization is a significant part and signature of Gulf car culture. Wealthy car owners frequently work with manufacturers or specialty shops to create unique versions of their luxury vehicles. Customization can range from personalized color schemes, special leather interiors, and advanced entertainment systems to rare materials like gold accents, Swarovski crystals, or custom emblems. Many locals take pride in creating cars that stand out, not only for the sake of luxury but also as a form of self-expression.

Specialty car shops and international brands often work with Gulf customers to create bespoke vehicles tailored to their specific tastes. Some carmakers even offer one-of-a-kind "designer editions" of their models exclusively in Gulf markets. These models feature unique touches like inlaid jewels, custom-paint jobs, and rare woods or fabrics sourced globally.

In addition to luxury sedans and supercars, the Gulf states have a deep-rooted culture around SUVs , Sports Cars and off-road vehicles. This interest stems from the region's unique terrain, which includes vast deserts ideal for dune bashing and other off-road activities. SUVs from brands like Toyota, Nissan, and Land Rover are commonly modified to withstand the rigors of dune bashing and desert driving.

SUVs and Crossovers and other larger vehicles are practical in the Gulf not only because of their suitability for desert conditions but also due to their comfort and size, making them popular among families. High-end models like the Range Rover, Mercedes-Benz G-Class, and Lexus LX are often favored for their luxurious interiors, durability, and off-road capabilities.

Dune-Bashing and Desert Rallying is considered an integral part of local desert culture. In fact dune-bashing has made modified SUVs and all-terrain vehicles (ATVs) highly sought after. Vehicles are often modified with lift kits, enhanced suspensions, and reinforced tires to handle the shifting sands. Toyota's Land Cruiser, in particular, is known for its desert reliability and remains a popular choice for desert driving and weekend expeditions .

The Gulf's car culture is further emphasized through numerous auto shows, car clubs, and racing events. The Dubai International Motor Show, for instance, is a major event where high-end carmakers showcase their latest models, and exclusive unveilings are often reserved for Gulf audiences. Car clubs, meanwhile, provide a social outlet for car enthusiasts, who gather for group drives, rallies, and exhibitions.

Motorsports also have a prominent place in Gulf culture, with highly viewed Formula 1 races held in Bahrain and Abu Dhabi, where fans gather to witness high-speed races and luxury car parades. These events serve as a testament to the Gulf's passion for fast cars and high-octane entertainment, further reinforcing the significance of car culture .

As the world moves toward sustainable energy, the Gulf states have stepped up and started to explore electric and hybrid luxury vehicles. Though it might seem paradoxical, the high demand for electric vehicles (EVs) in the Gulf has encouraged brands like Tesla, Lucid Motors, and Porsche to introduce their EV models to the market. For example, the UAE and Saudi Arabia are making significant investments in EV infrastructure and green energy, indicating that luxury car buyers may soon be considering electric supercars alongside traditional gas-powered options.

The Gulf states' vehicle culture is one of extravagance, high performance, and personal expression. With high-end brands, customization options, and a strong influence from off-road and motorsport activities, cars in the Gulf go beyond utility in that they represent a lifestyle. As the region adapts to new trends like sustainability, the Gulf's car culture will likely evolve, adding more innovative and eco-conscious options to the wide array of vehicles already present. For now, though, the blend of luxury, tradition, and modernity continues to make Gulf car culture one of the most distinctive in the world.

For daily life of expats however , multitudes of affordable vehicle options are available for work or family use . Cars made in Japan , US , France and Korea dominate the market . Several buying options are available either through direct purchase , trade ins , hire purchase or car loans . Although the process of obtaining a driving license is somewhat difficult in Gulf States , these facilities and the relatively affordable prices of cars in the Gulf States , are made use of extensively by the expat population .

CHAPTER 16

GROCERY CULTURE

A brief look into the Grocery Shopping Culture in the Gulf States. With High-End Supermarkets, Cooperative Societies, and Food Subsidies the choice of outlets for everyday purchases in the Gulf countries are very extensive . In the Gulf states, grocery shopping goes beyond just meeting daily needs; it's an integral part of lifestyle, convenience, and social experience. This region, characterized by high standards of living and cosmopolitan tastes, offers a unique array of grocery options that reflect the diversity of its population and the influence of globalization.

From luxurious, high-end supermarkets offering premium products to government-run cooperative societies providing essential goods at subsidized prices, the Gulf offers a rich, varied grocery shopping experience. This chapter examines the supermarket landscape in the Gulf, including high-end stores, government cooperatives, and the impact of food subsidies on local communities.

High-End Supermarket Chains cater to a Cosmopolitan Population . The Gulf's high-end supermarkets serve a diverse population of locals, expatriates, and high-income residents. These supermarkets often emphasize international quality, luxury products, and a shopping experience that prioritizes convenience and ambiance.

Some of the most prominent high-end grocery chains in the Gulf include the Waitrose (Only in UAE, Qatar) . Known for its British heritage and premium goods, Waitrose has established itself as a popular choice among expatriates and locals who value high-quality products. The supermarket is known for its range of organic produce, international products, and gourmet items that appeal to discerning shoppers.

Spinneys (Only in UAE, Oman) . Often regarded as the go-to supermarket for premium goods, Spinneys is known for offering a mix of local and international products. It stocks items from specialty foods to high-quality meats and cheeses, catering to shoppers who value quality. Spinneys is also known for its ready-to-eat gourmet foods, imported delicacies, and an extensive bakery section.

Lulu Hypermarket (Presence in All GCC countries) . Though Lulu Hypermarket caters to a broad range of income levels, its flagship stores feature high-end sections, particularly in major Gulf cities like Dubai, Riyadh, and Doha. Lulu offers an impressive variety of imported foods from India, the United States, the UK, and more, appealing to expatriates and locals alike. It's also popular for its expansive range of fresh produce, seafood, and meats.

Carrefour (Presence in All GCC countries) A French multinational chain, Carrefour has become a household name in the Gulf. While not exclusively a high-end supermarket, its "Carrefour Market" stores cater to shoppers looking for quality products in a premium setting. Carrefour often features a wide range of fresh produce, specialty foods, and organic options, in addition to international brands.

Choithrams (Only in UAE, Bahrain, Oman): This Indian-origin chain is known for its premium products and stocks a mix of international and regional goods, including British, Indian, and Arab products. Choithrams appeals to high-income shoppers seeking specialty foods and international brands, with an emphasis on quality and variety.

These popular supermarkets often occupy prime locations within large malls or high-end residential areas, offering shoppers a seamless experience with access to parking, in-store dining, and premium services like delivery and personal shopping. High-end supermarkets in the Gulf also distinguish themselves by offering diverse product selections, such as organic and gluten-free items, specialty cheeses, imported meats, artisanal chocolates, and gourmet coffee. This diversity reflects the Gulf's multicultural society, catering to the tastes and dietary preferences of residents from around the world.

Government-Owned Cooperative Societies on the other hand ensures Affordability and Access for the medium income expatriates and locals . Alongside high-end supermarkets, government-run cooperative societies play a critical role in the grocery landscape of the Gulf. These cooperatives are particularly common in the UAE, Kuwait, and Qatar, where they were established to ensure affordable access to essential goods and to stabilize prices for key commodities. By offering a basic range of necessities at subsidized rates, cooperative societies help keep living costs manageable, particularly for local families and lower-income households.

Union Coop (Operates in UAE) . Union Coop is one of the largest consumer cooperatives in the UAE, offering a wide range of food and non-food items at discounted prices. It focuses on keeping prices affordable for UAE nationals and residents, with a special emphasis on staple goods. Union Coop operates both large hypermarkets and neighborhood convenience stores, making affordable grocery options accessible in various parts of the country.

Al Meera (Operates in Qatar) . Qatar's national cooperative, Al Meera, is supported by the government to ensure food security and access to affordable groceries. Al Meera supermarkets are widely available across Qatar, and the chain's pricing policies aim to make essential goods accessible to the general population. They stock both local and international products to cater to Qatar's diverse population, often at competitive prices.

Kuwait Cooperative Society (Operates in Kuwait) . Established in the 1960s, Kuwait's cooperative societies are among the oldest in the Gulf. Each neighborhood typically has its own co-op store, which acts as a social and community hub for residents. These stores offer essential items and groceries at lower prices, with regular discounts on subsidized goods such as rice, sugar, flour, and cooking oil. Kuwait's co-ops also promote local produce, helping support national agriculture and sustainability.

All these Cooperatives play a crucial role in ensuring food security, particularly during times of crisis. For example, during the COVID-19 pandemic, these cooperatives played a key role in stabilizing food supplies and managing panic buying. Many cooperative societies have also adopted modern retail practices, offering online shopping options, loyalty programs, and delivery services to cater to evolving customer expectations.

Food Subsidies in the Gulf supports local economies and reduces living costs for its nationals . Food subsidies in the Gulf are a significant element of the grocery shopping landscape, with governments providing financial support to make staple items affordable for their citizens. These subsidies often cover essential goods such as rice, flour, sugar, milk, and cooking oil. In some cases, subsidies also extend to products like baby formula, ensuring that basic nutritional needs are met without placing undue financial pressure on families.

The UAE provides food subsidies to Emirati nationals, particularly on essential goods like rice, flour, and sugar. These items are available at a reduced cost through cooperative societies like Union Coop. The government has also implemented food security initiatives to promote local production and reduce dependency on imports.

Saudi Arabia provides subsidies on basic goods such as wheat and flour, ensuring affordability for Saudi families. Additionally, the government has developed programs to boost local agriculture, particularly in dairy and poultry, to increase domestic food security. The recent trend towards "Vision 2030" has seen a push for more locally produced food to reduce dependence on imports, with subsidies supporting this shift.

Kuwait and Qatar both have well-established food subsidy programs, providing items like rice, milk, and other essentials at reduced prices for citizens. Kuwait's cooperative societies offer these subsidized items, while Qatar has similar policies through Al Meera and other outlets.

Food subsidies not only support citizens in managing living costs but also help regulate the market. They allow governments to control the prices of key goods, preventing price inflation and ensuring that essential items remain within reach of all citizens. Subsidies and cooperative societies together create a balanced grocery shopping environment in the Gulf, where luxury and affordability coexist, providing options for a wide range of income levels.

Specialty and online grocery shopping trends have surged in the Gulf countries lately . As Gulf residents become more accustomed to convenience, technology, and niche dietary needs, online grocery shopping has surged in popularity. Platforms like Instashop, Carrefour Online, and Lulu's e-commerce platform have seen significant growth, offering delivery options that make grocery shopping easy and accessible . Additionally, specialty stores have emerged to cater to growing demand for organic, health-conscious, and gourmet products. Stores like Organic Foods and Café and specialized online platforms like Kibsons (Only in UAE) provide organic produce, vegan items, and specialty diet foods to customers looking for niche products not always available in traditional supermarkets.

The grocery shopping landscape in the Gulf reflects the region's unique blend of affluence, government support, and cosmopolitan tastes. High-end supermarkets cater to the Gulf's well-heeled residents, offering premium products and global brands, while government-owned cooperative societies and food subsidies ensure that essential goods remain affordable and accessible to all. Together, these shopping options create a rich and varied grocery experience, reflective of both the region's luxury lifestyle and its commitment to food security and accessibility. As the Gulf states continue to embrace technology and evolve their retail practices, grocery shopping in the region will likely become even more dynamic, balancing luxury with practicality to serve a diverse population.

CHAPTER 17

COFFEE CULTURE IN THE GULF

Coffee Culture in the Gulf States is truly a blend of tradition and modernity .The Gulf States have a deeply rooted and evolving coffee culture that bridges both local traditions and international influences. Coffee is far more than a beverage in these regions. It is a symbol of hospitality, social gatherings, and cultural pride. Over recent decades, this tradition has blended with the wave of modern international coffee culture, creating a unique fusion that appeals to both locals and expats. This chapter explores the elements of Gulf coffee culture, from traditional Arabic coffee ceremonies to the influence of Western-style cafes and specialty coffee movements.

All over the Gulf countries one will be enthralled by the traditional Arabic Coffee (Qahwa) Culture . Origins and Symbolism of Arabic coffee, or qahwa, has been integral to the Gulf region for centuries. It symbolizes warmth, generosity, and hospitality. Offering coffee to a guest is a deep-rooted gesture of respect and welcome, often accompanied by dates or sweets. Historically, coffee culture in the Gulf has its roots in Bedouin tribes, where majlis (a social gathering space) was where coffee was brewed and shared. The drink was prepared and served as a ritual, with a focus on honor, patience, and hospitality.

The Process and Presentation of Arabic coffee is unique to the Guif region . Traditional Arabic coffee is prepared using lightly roasted green coffee beans and a blend of spices such as cardamom, saffron, and sometimes even cloves. The coffee is brewed in a dallah (a traditional Arabic coffee pot) and served in small handle-less cups called finjan. Only a very small amount is poured at a time, and guests usually have the option of drinking up to three servings.

It is customary for the guest to signal they are finished by shaking the empty cup.

Social Customs and the Majlis are entwined in the Gulf . The majlis, a space dedicated to socializing, is where the essence of coffee culture truly shines. In Gulf society, this area has been crucial to community life and social discourse, serving as a place for sharing stories, business discussions, and hospitality. Even today, many homes and establishments have designated majlis areas, maintaining this aspect of coffee culture. The sharing of coffee fosters a sense of unity and respect within the group.

The Rise of International Coffee Influence has also had a huge impact in the Gulf countries. The arrival of International Coffee Chains revolutionized the coffee culture . The Gulf states having experienced rapid modernization and urbanization in the late 20th century, witnessed a surge of Western brands and lifestyles. International coffee chains like Starbucks, Costa Coffee, and Tim Hortons quickly became popular in cities across the region, especially in the UAE and Saudi Arabia. These coffee shops were not only places to enjoy coffee but became gathering spots mostly for youth, professionals, and expatriates.

This western Café Culture Evolution resonated with Gulf residents, especially the younger generations and expatriates, who sought spaces that blended global trends with local social needs. Coffee shops became hubs for socializing, studying, working, and meeting friends. Unlike traditional majlis customs, international cafés introduced an accessible, informal environment with free internet where people could meet at any time of day . Now almost every office tower typically has its own coffee shop .

Aesthetic Appeal and Social Media also plays a large part in the coffee culture . Instagrammable cafés and coffee presentations have become particularly influential, with Gulf coffee shops often featuring eye-catching décor, unique furniture, and photogenic beverages. With high smartphone penetration in the region, social media has fueled a rise in artisanal cafés, where visual appeal and quality coffee are celebrated. This has led to cafés becoming more than just a coffee spot , they have become social landmarks in cities across the Gulf.

The Specialty Coffee Movement arose with a high demand for high quality coffee beans and brewing techniques. Inspired by international trends, Gulf coffee enthusiasts including expats are increasingly interested in specialty coffee focusing on premium beans, quality roasting, and precise brewing techniques. Specialty cafés that prioritize single-origin beans and alternative brewing methods have flourished, especially in cities like Dubai, Riyadh, and Doha.

The Gulf has witnessed the rise of local coffee roasters and homegrown brands committed to high-quality, ethically sourced coffee beans. These homegrown brands are carving a niche by appealing to both locals and expats who are passionate about specialty coffee. Cafés such as Seven Fortunes in Dubai and Nabati Coffee in Riyadh focus on crafting coffee with locally inspired flavors, attracting a loyal following.

Coffee-related events, including barista competitions, coffee festivals, and brewing workshops, are also gaining popularity in the Gulf. Events like the Dubai International Coffee & Tea Festival and the Middle East Coffee Championships have drawn in global and regional talent, establishing the Gulf as a competitive and skilled coffee market.

This Cultural Fusion is no easy feat . Merging Local and Global Influences and blending Arabic and Western Coffee Styles into the Gulf coffee scene happened Gradually but decisively. A unique aspect of Gulf coffee culture today is the fusion of traditional Arabic coffee with contemporary flavors and presentation styles. Some specialty cafés now offer modern interpretations of qahwa or traditional brews paired with innovative desserts. This blend allows the Gulf's coffee culture to retain its heritage while appealing to the changing tastes of younger generations.

Café Design and Ambience is famed throughout the Gulf . Cafés in the Gulf are known for their stylish interiors, often blending Arabic motifs with minimalist, modern design. Many cafés use local art, Arabic calligraphy, and cultural symbols in their decor, bridging global coffee trends with the region's rich cultural heritage. The atmosphere of these cafés appeals to a broad audience, allowing them to cater to both traditional gatherings and casual .

As in other parts of the world, Gulf coffee consumers are increasingly aware of sustainability and ethical sourcing. Many cafés and roasters are committed to sourcing beans from fair-trade farms and practicing sustainable roasting techniques. This commitment reflects the Gulf's growing focus on environmental responsibility and aligns the region's coffee culture with global sustainability trends.

The coffee culture in the Gulf States is a dynamic blend of tradition and modernity. While deeply rooted in the customs of Arabic coffee ceremonies, it has evolved to incorporate international influences and specialty coffee movements. Gulf cities today offer a diverse coffee experience, from traditional qahwa ceremonies to hip, minimalist cafés where the latest trends in specialty coffee are embraced. This fusion has allowed coffee to become not only a symbol of hospitality but also a significant cultural and social experience, bridging the region's past with its future.

As the Gulf continues to modernize, the coffee culture will likely further adapt, retaining the heritage of qahwa while embracing new, globalized perspectives on coffee enjoyment.

CHAPTER 18

A chapter outlining two notable sites in each of the six Gulf states:

The Gulf Cooperation Council (GCC) countries—Bahrain, Kuwait, Oman, Qatar, Saudi Arabia, and the United Arab Emirates , offer a captivating blend of tradition and modernity. Here, we explore two notable sites in each of these countries, each reflecting the unique character, history, and aspirations of the Gulf.

1. Bahrain
   Bahrain Fort (Qal'at al-Bahrain)
   Situated on the northern coast of Bahrain Island, the Bahrain Fort is a UNESCO World Heritage Site that dates back to 2300 BCE. This archaeological site reveals layers of Bahrain's history from the Dilmun civilization, through the Persian and Islamic periods, to more recent Portuguese occupation. Visitors can explore ancient city remains, walls, and a museum that contextualizes the fort's importance to Gulf history.
   Al Fateh Grand Mosque
   As one of the largest mosques in the world, the Al Fateh Grand Mosque is an architectural marvel with its immense fiberglass dome, Italian marble, and Austrian glass. Open to visitors, it offers a chance to explore Islamic art, architecture, and culture, providing insights into Bahrain's spiritual life.

2. Kuwait

Kuwait Towers

The iconic Kuwait Towers, symbolizing modern Kuwait, are a testament to Kuwait's journey towards modernization. These towers, a blend of spherical shapes and Islamic design, provide panoramic views of the city and the Persian Gulf from observation decks, making it a must-visit for those seeking a blend of architectural wonder and scenic beauty.

Tareq Rajab Museum

This private museum holds a rich collection of Islamic art and cultural artifacts from across the Islamic world. Exhibits range from manuscripts and textiles to jewelry and ceramics, giving visitors a unique perspective on Islamic heritage and Kuwaiti culture.

3. Oman

Sultan Qaboos Grand Mosque

Located in Muscat, this grand mosque, built from Indian sandstone, is a masterpiece of Islamic architecture. Known for its massive prayer hall, intricate chandelier, and stunning Persian carpet, it welcomes visitors to learn about Oman's religious traditions and admire its craftsmanship.

Nizwa Fort

Built in the 17th century, Nizwa Fort offers a glimpse into Oman's history as a center for education, trade, and religion. With its robust defenses and towering walls, the fort highlights traditional Omani architecture, while exhibits within the fort provide insights into Omani life, weaponry, and local crafts.

4. Qatar

The Museum of Islamic Art

Situated on Doha's waterfront, the Museum of Islamic Art is designed by world-renowned architect I. M. Pei. The museum houses a vast collection of Islamic art spanning over a thousand years and multiple continents. The architecture itself is awe-inspiring, symbolizing Qatar's commitment to cultural preservation.

Souq Waqif

This bustling marketplace is a cultural hub in Doha. Renovated to preserve its historical ambiance, Souq Waqif offers an array of traditional goods, from spices and perfumes to handcrafted garments. It's a place where visitors can experience Qatar's rich traditions and lively market culture.

5. Saudi Arabia

Al-Ula (Hegra)

Recognized as Saudi Arabia's first UNESCO World Heritage Site, Al-Ula's ancient city of Hegra , is known for its Nabatean tombs carved into sandstone cliffs, much like Petra in Jordan. This archaeological wonder reveals Saudi Arabia's ancient past and its significance on the Arabian trade routes.

The Edge of the World

A popular attraction near Riyadh, the Edge of the World offers breathtaking views of the rocky desert landscape that stretches seemingly endlessly. This geological formation attracts adventurous travelers and provides a rare opportunity to experience Saudi Arabia's natural beauty.

6. United Arab Emirates (UAE)

Sheikh Zayed Grand Mosque

In Abu Dhabi, the Sheikh Zayed Grand Mosque stands as a symbol of tolerance and inclusiveness. Known for its stunning white marble structure, intricate mosaics, and grand domes, this mosque is among the largest in the world and welcomes visitors of all faiths to experience its architectural beauty.

Burj Khalifa

As the tallest building in the world, the Burj Khalifa in Dubai , UAE it is an architectural marvel that showcases the UAE's modern ambitions. Standing at an impressive height of 828 meters (2,717 feet), it has 163 floors above ground and was completed in 2010. The Burj Khalifa features a mix of residential, commercial, and hotel spaces, as well as observation decks with panoramic views of Dubai. Its construction was a landmark achievement and solidified Dubai's status as a global center of innovation and architectural ambition. Visitors can ascend to the observation decks for a panoramic view of Dubai's skyline and surrounding desert, highlighting the country's transformation and rapid development.

Each of these sites offers a unique insight into the diverse heritage, culture, and aspirations of the Gulf states. From ancient fortresses to modern marvels, they reflect a region rich in history, faith, and progress, inviting visitors to explore its multifaceted identity.

CONCLUSION

Life in the Gulf states is a fascinating blend of ancient traditions and dynamic modernity, where rich cultural heritage coexists with cutting-edge innovation. In the cities, towering skyscrapers and vast shopping malls contrast with the timeless rhythm of traditional souqs and historic districts. While rapid development has transformed these nations into global hubs, Gulf societies remain deeply rooted in values of family, hospitality, and spirituality.

The warm desert landscapes, coupled with the bustling energy of cosmopolitan centers, reflect a way of life that embraces both past and future. As these states continue to evolve, they offer an inspiring model of resilience, adaptation, and ambition, drawing people from around the world to witness and participate in a truly unique region bridging history and progress. The Gulf is timelessly enchanting and mysterious and will offer you beautiful memories to cherish all your life .

R.M.

The author , Ms. Mendez , is of Portuguese ancestry and Anglo Indian origin . She holds a Masters in Aviation from Switzerland , and currently lives in the Middle East . The author can be reached on email hellorishimendez@gmail.com

About the Author

The author Ms.Mendez of Portugese descent , and Anglo Indian origin , is an Aviation professional living in the Middle East .